Ethiopia, The Horn of Africa, and U.S. Policy

John H. Spencer

Foreign Policy Report
September 1977

INSTITUTE FOR FOREIGN POLICY ANALYSIS, INC.
Cambridge, Massachusetts

Requests for copies of IFPA Foreign Policy Reports should be addressed to the Circulation Manager, Foreign Policy Reports, Institute for Foreign Policy Analysis, Inc., Central Plaza Building, Tenth Floor, 675 Massachusetts Avenue, Cambridge, Massachusetts 02139. (Telephone: 617-492-2116) Please send a check or money order for the correct amount along with your order.

Standing orders for all Foreign Policy Reports will be accepted by the Circulation Manager. Standing order subscribers will automatically receive all future Reports as soon as they are published. Each Report will be accompanied by an invoice.

IFPA also maintains a **mailing list** of individuals and institutions who are notified periodically of new Institute publications. Those desiring to be placed on this list should write to the Circulation Manager, Foreign Policy Reports, at the above address.

Manuscripts should be submitted to the Managing Editor, Foreign Policy Reports, at the above address. They should be typed double-spaced; footnotes, also double-spaced, should be placed at the end. Manuscripts should be from 80 to 120 pages, or from 20,000 to 30,000 words, in length. Those not accepted for publication will be returned only if adequate postage has been provided by the author.

A list of IFPA publications appears on the inside back cover.

The Institute for Foreign Policy Analysis, Inc., incorporated in the Commonwealth of Massachusetts in 1976, is a publicly-supported, nonprofit, tax-exempt corporation, as described in Section 501(c)(3) of the Internal Revenue Code. Contributions to the Institute are tax-deductible.

Price: $5.00

Library of Congress Catalog No. 77-87562

ISBN 0-89549-005-6

First Printing
Printed by Corporate Press, Inc., Washington, D.C.

Contents

1.
Introduction

DIPLOMATIC BARGAINING over the future of Rhodesia, the invasion of Zaire, the actions of Idi Amin, the continuing international debate over *Apartheid* in South Africa, Cuban intervention in Angola, Soviet inroads in various parts of Africa—all these headline issues have tended to obscure ominous and equally critical developments in the Horn of Africa, where the oil-tanker lanes from the Persian Gulf to the West and to the Suez Canal intersect. In recent years the United States, retreating before the advance of the Soviet Union, has lost the dominant position of strength and prestige it held in this region throughout the 1950s and 1960s. The formerly strong British presence throughout the Red Sea and the Gulf of Aden is only a memory. The recent departure of France from the strategic port of Djibouti—the last colonial territory in Africa—now threatens to throw the entire Horn into turmoil, from which only the Soviets can profit. In pace with these changes, the United States has closed down its defense installations in Ethiopia at the same time that the Soviet Union has been consolidating, at nearby Berbera in Marxist Somalia, the largest Soviet-controlled missile, naval and air base outside the Warsaw Pact countries.

To a remarkable degree, the future course of developments in northeast Africa will be determined by the fate of Ethiopia, which is the source of water for the entire region, including the lower Nile. Her destiny is, today, in considerable doubt because of the great internal and external disruptions following the 1974 revolution which overthrew the pro-Western rule of Haile Sellassie I.

It is extraordinary that a dictatorship, which came to power through widespread dissatisfaction with the crumbling monarchical regime, could have become within three years the target of fear, hatred and opposition from almost every significant segment of Ethiopian society. A bare sketch of the more articulate centers of opposition—proceeding ideologically from left to right—suggests the depth and magnitude of the dissent:

Marxist EPRP (Ethiopian People's Revolutionary Party)

students

labor unions

bureaucracy[1]

---

[1] For the recent campaign against the bureaucracy, see *Ethiopian Herald* (Addis Ababa), December 25, 1976, p. 2 ("Bureaucracy is the illegitimate child of imperialism"); and January 14, 1977, p. 2 ("Bureaucracy is a product of bourgeois capitalism and industrialism").

ELF (Eritrean Liberation Front), and to a lesser degree the EPLF (Eritrean People's Liberation Front)

Tigre Liberation Front and the Tigre Popular Liberation Forces

Oromo Liberation Front

air force[2]

provincial police[2]

peasants, who are refusing to plant crops by way of protest against the nationalization of farm lands

trading communities, which are refusing to stockpile goods because of the nationalization and antihoarding policies of the government (the Derg)

the Right, represented by the EDU (Ethiopian Democratic Union)

It is equally remarkable that the EPRP and the EDU, ideological enemies but both partisans of a united Ethiopia, have now been able to join with the ELF, the protagonist of Eritrean secession, to form an alliance for the purpose of bringing down the Derg.[3]

Faced with nationwide hostility and violence, the Derg responded in four ways. First, to politicize the masses it established two agencies: the Political Office for Mass Organizational Affairs and the Yekatit 66 Ideological School, both under Haile Fida, Head of the Politburo and of the All Ethiopia Socialist Movement. Then, in order to control and curb the power of this principal political officer, the Head of State, Lt. Colonel Mangistu Haile Mariam, created a military group called the *Seded* (Fire of the Revolution). Later the Derg set up local urban associations of citizens supplied with arms, called *kebele*, largely for the purpose of liquidating the EPRP. Still later, it established a Congress of all Derg members (about sixty) whose function it is to elect the forty members of the Central Committee which, in turn, elects the Permanent Committee of Seventeen, presided over by Head of State Mangistu.

Second, the Derg proclaimed the Soviet doctrine of "unity in diversity" with specific application to the disaffected Galla (the large ethnic group, rival to the dominant Amhara) in the south and west.[4]

Third, following the established tradition of juntas, the Derg reacted with a policy of mass arrests and executions, now numbering in the thousands. "House-cleanings" held in July, October and November of 1976 as a sequel to the mass executions of November 1974, were themselves followed by the execution on February 3, 1977, of the Head of

---

[2] See *Le Monde*, December 31, 1976.

[3] *Ethiopian Herald*, December 19, 23, 26, 1976; January 14, 1977, p. 2; *New York Times*, December 11, 1976; February 1, 2, 10, 1977.

[4] *Ethiopian Herald*, December 17, 19, 28, 1976, January 13, 14, 1977.

State, General Teferi Bante, and other senior officials[5] suspected of seeking compromises over Eritrea and of wanting to come to terms with the EPRP.[6] The following day, the new Chief of State, Lt. Colonel Mangistu, called for a reign of terror against all elements of resistance.[7]

Fourth, the Derg's February proclamation of terror was accompanied by the announcement that Ethiopia no longer had friends, only enemies, except for the Marxist People's Democratic Republic of Yemen—a statement that gave one the feeling that he was witnessing the crises of the year 1793, when a February declaration of war against Great Britain, Holland and Spain ushered in the Reign of Terror in France. Ethiopia's longstanding friend, the Sudan, now became the target of bitter attacks; even sharper accusations and mass demonstrations against "CIA plots" proclaimed the regime's hostility toward the United States, which, for nearly a quarter of a century, had been the source of Ethiopia's military assistance.[8] While no African state, except Libya, felt moved to send congratulations to the Derg on the February 3rd liquidations, several communist countries did, namely, the Soviet Union, Yugoslavia, the People's Republic of China, the People's Democratic Republic of Yemen, and Cuba.

Thus, by early 1977 Ethiopia had made a clean break with the past and was moving into a new orbit. The two basic questions about her future are whether she will actually enter the communist bloc and whether she will survive as an entity, given the steadily mounting successes of the secessionists in Eritrea and of Somali infiltrators in Ethiopia's southeastern province of the Ogaden.

Critical to Ethiopia's future is the Greater Somaliland Movement based in Marxist Somalia, now largely a client state of the Soviet Union. Since the beginning of the twentieth century, first Italy, then the British, and now Somalia herself, have sought to annex the Ogaden to Somalia. Its water and grazing resources were and are considered essential to the well-being of the nomadic populations of Somalia's wastelands.[9] The fascist invasion and the Italo-Ethiopian War in the 1930s started there. From 1943 onward, the Greater Somaliland Movement called for the annexation of the Ogaden, and of the French territory of Djibouti as well, to Somalia.

---

[5] Lt. Colonel Asrat Desta, Captain Moges Wolde Michael and Captain Alemayehu Haile of the Standing Committee of Seventeen, the name given to the Politburo following the reorganization at the end of 1976. See *ibid.*, December 30, 1976.

[6] See *Africa Confidential*, January 7, 1977, p. 1, and May 13, 1977, p. 3.

[7] *Washington Post*, February 11, 1977, p. A-14. Mangistu promised "to create terror in their camps as they did in ours." *Le Monde (Sélection hebdomadaire)*, "Combattre la terreur par la terreur," February 7, 1977.

[8] One of the numerous complaints against the Derg was that it was plotting with Khaddafi of Libya the abortive coup of July 1976 against Sudan's ruler, Nimeiri. On the availability of arms from Eastern Europe, see the *Washington Post*, February 12, 1977, p. A-9.

[9] This area is of equal importance to both the former Italian and British Somalilands that were united in 1960 to form the independent state of Somalia.

The independence of the Djibouti territory on June 27, 1977, and the consistent refusal of Somalia to agree in advance to respect that independence, make it clear that the Movement remains the prime concern of Somali policies.

The Soviets have gradually converted Somalia into a client state, supplying her with financial and economic aid, an ambitious drought relief program, and weapons, planes, tanks, transport and training that now exceed those made available to Ethiopia by the United States. Some 2,000 Soviet "technicians" and military advisers are present, ready to assist if that military strength is employed in some foreign adventure. The turmoil in Ethiopia, the failure of the Derg to master the revolt in the province of Eritrea, the hostility of Ethiopia's neighbors, and the certainty that neither the Organization of African Unity (OAU) nor the United Nations would intervene—all these factors present Somali leaders with an almost irresistible temptation to "liberate" the Ogaden and thus to realize a goal sought for three-quarters of a century.

So long as the Soviets were seeking to gain control over the Derg, it was important for them to keep in check the Greater Somaliland Movement of their client state, Somalia. Once that control had been achieved, it became equally important to allow violence to erupt in the Ogaden so as to convince Mogadiscio that Soviet control over Somalia's traditional enemy was in no way incompatible with the USSR's alliance with Somalia. The series of liquidations in Ethiopia, from June 1976 to February 1977, of lukewarm Soviet sympathizers; the pro-Soviet editorials of the controlled press; the protestations by the Derg that only the Marxist-Leninist states remain its friends; the Derg's anti-American propaganda and actions; the replacement of the United States by the USSR as the major arms supplier to Ethiopia—all reveal a desperate realization by the Derg that its survival, perhaps even that of Ethiopia, must now depend entirely upon the Soviet Union, for it is Moscow alone that can prevent the Somalis, under the banner of the Greater Somaliland Movement, from seizing the Ogaden and newly independent Djibouti, and that can also prevent the loss of Eritrea.

Unmistakable evidence of this capitulation to Soviet blackmail is to be found in the fact that Lt. Colonel Mangistu not only concluded an alliance agreement in Moscow,[10] but embraced the Soviet proposal for a federation of Ethiopia (including Eritrea), Somalia and the People's Democratic Republic of Yemen.[11] Swept into the Soviet orbit, Ethiopia called for the expulsion of all U.S. agencies except the Embassy,[12] ordered

---

[10] *New York Times*, May 6, p. A-3, and May 7, p. A-3, 1977.

[11] *Washington Post*, February 28, p. A-20, March 17, p. A-22, and March 18, p. A-19, 1977.

[12] The agencies closed down include the Kagnew Defense Installation, the Military Advisory Group, the U.S. Cultural Center, the U.S. Naval Research Unit, and the Consulate at Asmara.

the staff of the latter reduced by half, and recalled all students undergoing military training in the United States.

The retreat of the United States from the Horn to the remote Indian Ocean island of Diego Garcia—and there perhaps for only a short while—in response to Soviet advances in this strategically significant region, should be cause for concern to the United States and oil-thirsty Europe as well.

The purpose of this paper is to explore the causes and consequences of the American abandonment of the Horn of Africa and the Soviet succession to predominance in the area. We will examine the other regional and continental factors that account for this shift in superpower roles, the success of Moscow in transforming Somalia into a client state, the prospects for the Kremlin achieving the same results in Ethiopia, and the possibility that Ethiopia might lose some of her present territory. U.S. and Soviet interests in the region and their future policy options will also be treated. First, in the next several chapters, we will trace the growth of American influence in the region in the postwar period and the relations of Ethiopia with her neighbors during the reign of Haile Sellassie I.

The Ethiopian Character and Historical Experience

Before going on, it is important to consider briefly Ethiopia's unusual historical experience and its impact on the Ethiopian character. In dealing with Ethiopian problems, whether historically or in the present, one is confronted with a fortress mentality. By her size, population[13] and resources, Ethiopia dominates the Horn. Yet, at the same time, her fertile farming and grazing lands, temperate climate and strategic location on the shores of the Red Sea and its exit at the Strait of Bab el Mandeb have rendered her an attractive and vulnerable target. The source of all the water of Somalia and Djibouti and of 80 per cent of the waters of the lower Nile,[14] Ethiopia has been, throughout history, the object of covetous designs.[15]

---

[13] Ethiopia has 457,142 square miles, 27,140,000 inhabitants; Somalia has 246,155 square miles, 3,090,000 inhabitants.

[14] The recent four years of drought, shared with the Sahel, have been an unusual phenomenon. The traditional rainfall pattern has resumed this year.

[15] Much has been written pro and con about the campaigns of Menelik II who conquered parts of the modern state of Ethiopia, in particular the Ogaden. Certainly he and his successors treated the area as conquered territory. It was integrated into Ethiopia by force in the 1880s, but in much the same manner as the "Winning of the West" in North America, against warring tribes claiming identity only by agnate descent from some common male ancestor but acknowledging no nationality or other allegiance. (See I. M. Lewis, *A Pastoral Democracy* [London: Oxford University Press, 1961], p. 1.) Italy had no difficulty in purchasing the allegiance of the leaders of many such tribes. (See Robert L. Hess, *Italian Colonialism in Somalia* [Chicago, Ill.: Chicago University Press, 1966], pp. 25-33.) It was the Italian invasion of the Ogaden in 1934 that led to the Italian-Ethiopian War of 1935-1936, when the League of Nations determined Italy to have been the aggressor. The United States has subsequently consistently held the Ogaden to be an integral part of Ethiopia.

As the only independent country on the continent—except for Liberia—Ethiopia had been able to maintain her independence for centuries only by continually fighting off Arab forces and by playing off one rival colonial power against another. Whenever that policy could not be pursued, her independence was threatened.

During the first half of this century—the colonial period in Africa—those rivals were Britain, France and Italy, which surrounded her on all sides. However, the need to keep Fascist Italy from joining Nazi Germany led Britain and France at the Conference of Stresa in 1935 to abandon all rivalry for Ethiopia (a 1906 treaty had prospectively partitioned Ethiopia between the three powers) and to allow Italy a free hand there.[16] Before that year was out, Italy had attacked Ethiopia in the Ogaden which adjoins Somalia, then known as Italian Somaliland. A war with Italy ensued, and when Ethiopia appealed to the League of Nations, the struggling international organization was convulsed with a crisis from which it never recovered. Ethiopia was merged with Eritrea and Somalia into an Italian East Africa.

The end of colonialism in Africa and the Middle East in the postwar era has confronted Ethiopia with an even more dangerous peril. So long as the Arab territories were under colonial domination, the traditional hatred of Islamic peoples for Christian Ethiopia was kept under control. With the waning and ultimate disappearance of that rule, Arab attacks erupted, spurred on by the UN decision to return Eritrea—historically the oldest part of Ethiopia—with its Muslim minority, to Christian rule, and by the Arabs' distaste at seeing a Christian state installed on the western shores of "their" Red Sea. Those attacks continued to escalate over the years, until by 1974 a crisis of almost unmanageable proportions had arisen for Ethiopia.

It is this persistent pattern of foreign ambition and greed that has forced upon Ethiopia, whatever her faults and those of her people, a fortress situation and mentality. Indeed, from the seventeenth to the nineteenth century, Ethiopia, simultaneously with China and Japan and for similar reasons, cut herself off from foreign contacts. This siege mentality and outlook, forged by harsh experience, has over the years produced in the Ethiopian people a set of cultural characteristics that includes xenophobia, combativeness, obstinacy, arrogance, pretense (with foreign [farangi] and compatriot alike), irascibility, resourcefulness,

---

[16] In addition, France hoped that by allowing Italy to become entangled in Ethiopia, Italy might be hampered in prosecuting its ambitions in Tunisia. See Herbert Feis, *Seen From E.A.* (New York: Knopf, 1947), p. 199; George W. Baer, *The Coming of the Italian-Ethiopian War* (Cambridge, Mass.: Harvard University Press, 1967), pp. 118 ff; Lord Avon, *The Eden Memoirs: Facing the Dictators* (Boston, Mass.: Houghton Mifflin, 1962), pp. 200-239.

evasiveness, deviousness, loyalty, sardonic humor, subtlety, exquisite courtesy and cruelty.[17] In other words, Ethiopia is the *"animal méchant qui sait se défendre."*

The Ethiopian, whose language and origins are rooted in southern Arabia, remains possibly the most Asian of all African peoples south of the Sahara, in mentality, personality and outlook on the world. It is the combination of these conflicting traits of personality that account significantly for Ethiopia's remarkable ability to survive as an independent state in a hostile environment of warring satrapies and tribal chieftains.[18]

It has been the author's fortune to have been associated with Ethiopia's foreign affairs long enough to have witnessed the completion of a full forty-year cycle. In 1936, during the days of the League of Nations and the Italo-Ethiopian War, U.S.-Ethiopian relations were at a low point— when the United States sought to put as much political distance as possible between it and Ethiopia. These relations subsequently ascended to a high point midway in the cycle and remained there during much of the 1950s and 1960s, but now they have plummeted to total hostility.

---

[17] For a discussion of Ethiopian traits, see D. Levine, *Wax and Gold* (Chicago, Ill.: University of Chicago Press, 1965), pp. 248-253.

[18] "Les Ethiopiens, 'Asiatiques de l'Afrique,' rompus à l'art du complot et de la machination, donnent ici la pleine mesure de leur talent." J. C. Guillebaud, "La nouvelle 'énigme' éthiopienne," *Le Monde*, December 31, 1976.

2.
U.S.-Ethiopian Relations, 1935-1960

The Italo-Ethiopian War, 1935-1941

THE UNITED STATES was careful to avoid all involvement with Ethiopia in its struggle against the fascist invasion.[19] Washington rejected Haile Sellassie's request of July 3, 1935, to call upon Italy to respect the Kellogg-Briand (renunciation of war) Pact, and subsequently his appeal to the United States to serve as mediator. Secretary of State Cordell Hull required the Standard Vacuum Company to cancel its oil concession with Ethiopia lest, in the event of war, it should cause embarrassment to U.S. relations with the belligerents. When war did come, the United States declared that a state of war existed, thereby requiring under the neutrality legislation an embargo on the shipment of arms to both Ethiopia and Italy.[20] It also refrained from helping the League of Nations to apply sanctions against Italy and, following the fascist occupation of Ethiopia, declined the Emperor's request for a visit to the United States.

The Post-Liberation Period, 1941-1948

When Ethiopia was liberated in 1941, it was largely through British support in troops, arms and transport equipment that the Emperor, who had found exile in England, was able to lead his column of soldiers from the Sudan to Addis Ababa.[21] For the first year following liberation, all of

---

[19] Roosevelt remarked (July 26, 1935) that the Italo-Ethiopian dispute was of no concern to the United States. (Feis, p. 220.) "I appealed to him [Mussolini] in the ways which, as I understand him, are most apt to interest his understanding, sympathy, and support, with the hope that through those emotions might lie the way to induce him to consider some sort of compromise and pacific settlement.... I doubt if he had ever even in his own mind woven together all the elements of discord in Europe with the related problems of Africa. ... These were all woven together about Europe and Africa. The contributions to be made were that Italy should renounce some of her ambitions, even with the thought that the low-land tribes in Abyssinia might not consent and that he might have his little war anyhow." Ambassador Breckinridge Long to Secretary of State, September 17, 1935, *Foreign Relations of the United States*, 1935, Vol. I, p. 754. (Hereafter cited as *For. Rel.*). See also Bruce Harris, Jr., *The United States and the Italo-Ethiopian Crisis* (Stanford, Calif.: Stanford University Press, 1964), pp. 20-61.

[20] *For Rels.*, 1935, Vol. I, pp. 784-815. In his memoirs, *Facing the Dictators* (p. 424), Anthony Eden supports Sir Ronald Lindsay's impression that the United States had for some time lost interest in Ethiopia, and asserts that, unlike the British, French, Germans and others, the United States in the final stages of the war did not seek to dissuade Italy from bombing undefended towns. This last assertion would appear to be incorrect. It was not a reluctance to make such a *démarche*, but to make it jointly with others. Department of State to Ambassador in Italy, April 7, 1936, *For. Rels.*, 1936, Vol. III, p. 52.

[21] See G. L. Steer, *Sealed and Delivered* (London: Hodder and Stoughton, 1942); Lord Rennell of Rodd, *British Military Administration in Africa, 1941-1947* (London: HMSO, 1948), p. 327ff.

Ethiopia was under British military occupation. An agreement of January 31, 1942, ostensibly released most of Ethiopia from the occupation, with the exception of the Ogaden, the large area in the southeast where the war with Italy had started. Nevertheless, even liberated Ethiopia remained essentially under British control. British military units as part of the BMME (British Military Mission to Ethiopia) were present everywhere, as were British advisers. All communications, including the Emperor's personal correspondence, and air and surface transport, were controlled by them. Foreign airlines other than British were excluded. The East African shilling replaced the Italian lire and the traditional Ethiopian currency. Ethiopia was part of the sterling area. Goodyear, Goodrich or Firestone tires could be purchased only if they had been manufactured by their branches in England. All dollar exchange earned by exports had to be converted into pounds sterling. Traffic was moved from right to left and, under the agreement, the British Diplomatic Representative had precedence over his counterpart from any other state. At that time, the Department of State indicated to British Foreign Secretary Eden its concern over what was "tantamount to a protectorate over Abyssinia."[22]

Moreover, in addition to Ethiopia, the British had recovered British Somaliland from Italian occupation and assumed administration of all of Italian Somaliland and Eritrea. Thus, Britain controlled all of the Horn of Africa. Neighboring Kenya had remained under British rule. French Somaliland under the Vichy French was blockaded by British naval forces operating out of Aden. Under these circumstances, it was natural that the British, in contemplation of postwar settlements, should have developed the concept of a Greater (British) Somaliland, comprising parts of Kenya and Ethiopia (the Ogaden), and all of Italian, British and French Somalilands. France was to be compensated elsewhere for the loss of Djibouti. This concept was entirely exogenous in origin, making its appearance only after the British had assumed administration of the Horn. Somalia itself had never existed as a separate entity. Before the advent of the Italians, much of the coastal area was claimed by the Sultan of Zanzibar from whom Italy purchased the "Benadir Coast" by agreement in 1905 for the sum of £144,000, payments on which continued until 1937. Other areas were claimed by various sultans who readily sold themselves into Italian protection, such as the Sultan of Obbia.

A movement in support of Greater Somaliland began to take form in 1943 with the establishment in the Ogaden, under British military occu-

---

[22] Department of State (DOS) Memorandum, June 18, 1941, 884.001 Selassie I372; DOS Memorandum to President Roosevelt, July 24, 1942, 884.001 Selassie I 374/1/2; and Letter, Roosevelt to Winant, August 4, 1942, 844.001 Selassie I/375 PS/KN, National Archives. (Unless otherwise indicated, file numbers will hereinafter refer to National Archives file numbers.)

pation, of what became known as the Somali Youth League, largely under the leadership of Abdullahi Issa. From the outset this movement struck an ominous note for Ethiopia. It was from these territories, in the sixteenth century, that the Muslim warrior, Gragn, led his followers in a *jihad* (holy war) as far north as Lake Tana. In 1935 Ethiopia went to war in defense of the Ogaden when it was invaded by Italy.[23] The inclusion of French Somaliland and its port of Djibouti in the formula for a Greater Somaliland also held dire implications for Ethiopia. The closure of that port by the French to the importation of arms for Ethiopia's defense was the direct and immediate cause for her defeat in that war. In turn, that same movement made solution of another problem more urgent. With continued foreign rule over Djibouti, the return of Eritrea, lost to the Italians half a century before, became a crucial issue, for it alone offered Ethiopia the possibility of assured access to the sea. The threat of a Greater Somaliland from 1943 on and the related problem of Eritrea have lain at the heart of the crisis in the Horn of Africa.

The development of relations between Ethiopia and the United States, under these conditions, depended largely on the degree to which the British permitted contact with the outside world. Thus, the reopening of diplomatic relations between Washington and Addis Ababa in 1942 was not without obstacles. The only channel of communication with Ethiopian officials lay through the British Legation in the capital. Because the British preferred that U.S. representation in Ethiopia be limited to a consulate-general, negotiations for the re-establishment of a U.S. Legation had to be carried on elsewhere. Once the Department of State had approved the final arrangements for opening a legation, the problem still remained of forwarding notification to the Ethiopian officials in Addis Ababa. This meant passing the message through the British Legation there. The British Minister held the note until the United States, alerted by the prolonged absence of a reply, finally forced the Minister to release it to the Ethiopians.[24]

In May 1943, the Emperor sought permission to buy some U.S. Army surplus from the U.S. Army PX at Asmara. Again, the message had to

[23] The Italo-Ethiopian War of 1935-1936 arose out of the invasion of the Ogaden across the Ethiopian boundary with Italian Somaliland. Since Liberation that same issue has ceaselessly poisoned relations. Ethiopia has insisted upon, and Somalia has rejected, application of the Italo-Ethiopian Boundary Treaty of 1908 by which Ethiopia surrendered claims to large areas, particularly along the Juba river. In 1959 the United Nations took note of its inability to promote a settlement of the issue. See Saadia Touval, *Boundary Politics of Independent Africa* (Cambridge, Mass.: Harvard University Press, 1972), pp. 212-245; Ethiopian Ministry of Press and Information, *The Ethio-Somaliland Frontier* (Addis Ababa, 1961); Mesfin Wolde Mariam, "The Background of the Ethio-Somalian Boundary Dispute," *Journal of Modern African Studies*, Vol. II, No 2 (1964), pp. 189-219. Although the border with Kenya was established as a closed frontier—recently opened for grazing—Italy and Great Britain were able to impose on Ethiopia unilateral grazing privileges for their tribes from Italian and British Somalilands.

[24] Despatch Amlegation, Addis Ababa, February 18, 1943, 884.1121/2.

pass through the British Legation, which, instead of forwarding it to Asmara, sent it directly to Middle East Headquarters in Cairo. When contact was made with U.S. headquarters there, the latter agreed to turn over all military supplies in Asmara to the British, and then, through the British, informed the PX and the Emperor that no such supplies were available.[25] Eventually, the U.S. Legation in Addis Ababa was able to establish its own direct radio link with Washington.

In that same month, a special Ethiopian Mission was allowed to proceed to the United States to attend the World Food Conference held at Hot Springs, Virginia. Actually, the Conference served as a cover for an approach by the Ethiopian government to obtain lend-lease assistance, a governor for the State Bank of Ethiopia, and a legal adviser to assist in negotiating a new agreement to replace the 1942 Anglo-Ethiopian Agreement. Specifically, the Ethiopian government requested that the author return to the Ministry of Foreign Affairs where he had served as legal adviser during the Italo-Ethiopian War.[26]

During the last two years of the war and the immediate postwar years, the author's most important task was to negotiate with the British who seemed determined to keep a firm hand over the Horn, as illustrated by the following episode. In early 1945, when President Roosevelt decided to meet with Haile Sellassie at the Suez Canal on his return from Yalta, it was necessary to keep the plans totally secret from the British. Accordingly, the Emperor's unannounced departure, by U.S. military DC-3, was set for 5 a.m. No one, however, had counted on the keen sense of hearing and the insomnia of the British Minister, who, upon hearing the unusual sound of a take-off at five o'clock in the morning, jumped out of bed and, after finally learning what had happened, frantically sought a plane to rush him to Cairo. In the end, he had to settle for a tiny biplane out of Aden, which could make only short hops over the burning sands of the Sahara into Cairo. Before he left, he alerted Churchill, who suddenly found the prosecution of the war against Hitler less important than a trip to Cairo, although he did not take advantage of the occasion to meet with Roosevelt. The Emperor, who was upset that the British insisted on his seeing the Prime Minister after his meeting with Roosevelt, was asked by a British official what points he wished to bring up with Churchill. He replied "none." When the Prime Minister learned that Roosevelt had given Haile Sellassie some jeeps and command cars, he "upped the ante" by giving him a Rolls Royce.

---

[25] Despatch U.S. Consulate, Asmara, May 5, 1943, 884.24/105.

[26] The author refused, however, to assume his duties until approval of his appointment had been obtained from the British government. Article II(b) of the 1942 Agreement required consultation with the British government for the appointment of all non-British advisers.

Such were the conditions existing at the time the author was recalled to Ethiopia in the latter part of 1943. His first duty—one that had been specifically emphasized at the time of requesting his return—was to negotiate an agreement to replace that of 1942 so that Ethiopia could be released from what was, in fact if not in name, a British protectorate. This proved to be an exceptionally difficult assignment and one of considerable duration. It was only with the greatest trepidation that the Ethiopian government did finally take the step of denouncing the 1942 agreement, so as to force the British to agree to fresh negotiations. All sorts of possible reprisals were conjectured.

By far the most difficult problem encountered during the negotiations was the British insistence upon retaining the Ogaden. The British positively refused to return that area to Ethiopia (about one-third of the entire country) which they had retained under the 1942 agreement. Their insistence was based on the following argument: The British (unlike the United States with its nonrecognition policy) had recognized the fascist conquest of Ethiopia. Therefore, Ethiopia, although liberated, legally was enemy-occupied territory. In accordance with a British-Soviet-American agreement, the Ogaden, along with all enemy-occupied territories, was to be kept under military occupation until a peace settlement. In the meantime, the war must be pursued, and since the Ogaden was necessary for the prosecution of the war effort against Germany and Japan, the British must remain in occupation of that part of Ethiopia.

The Ethiopian government replied that, since it had been the first to enter the war against the Axis and to fight unaided against fascist aggression, and had already adhered to the Atlantic Charter, no part of its territory should be considered enemy-occupied territory. However, if the Ogaden was, in fact, necessary for the pursuit of the war against Germany and Japan, and if the United States, then engaged with Britain in the campaign in Western Europe and carrying the bulk of the effort in the Pacific, should also agree that the Ogaden was important to the Allied war effort, then, as a loyal ally, Ethiopia would agree to allow the British to remain there in occupation until the end of the war. The Ethiopian government felt itself compelled to hold fast to that position, since the Ogaden figured prominently in the British Greater Somaliland project. Upon receiving the response of the Ethiopian government, the British delegation "hit the ceiling," taking particular umbrage at the reference to the American war effort. The delegation then orally informed the Ethiopian government that, if it persisted in its attitude, the British might be compelled to re-occupy all of Ethiopia.

The American Minister in Addis Ababa, who had been kept informed of all details of the negotiations, reported the crisis to the Department of State and inquired regarding the position he should take on the matter.

The Department responded that there was nothing it could do about the situation beyond expressing to the British dissatisfaction with their actions which created the impression abroad that they were trying to take territory away from Ethiopia.[27]

In the end, faced with the threat of military reoccupation, Ethiopia had to give in to British demands. She did so under a formula by which, as an ally and as a contribution to the war effort, she consented that the Ogaden should remain under British military administration for the duration of the agreement. Against the possibility of a subsequent oil concession, the Ethiopian government obtained the reservation to itself of all subsoil rights. When the British finally realized what they had agreed to, they reneged on their commitment and insisted upon, and by exercising additional pressure obtained surrender to them of, subterranean water rights ostensibly for the pastoral tribes. In reality, as the Ethiopian government fully realized at the time, the British were seeking to establish a formula for obstructing any future oil exploration.

While many of the legal controls provided by the 1942 agreement, over courts, advisers, currency and aviation, were relaxed by the new agreement of 1944, most of them still continued to operate, to stifle postwar development, and to restrict the freedom of the U.S. government to provide assistance. Even during the war and before the conclusion of the 1944 agreement, the United States had viewed with favor a policy of assistance to Ethiopia. Among the factors promoting such a policy were the considerations that Ethiopia was at the time the only independent country in Africa, apart from Liberia; that it was considered "black" and consequently of political significance; that aid to Ethiopia as the "first to be freed" from Axis aggression could serve as encouragement to the many countries still under nazi occupation to join in the struggle against the Axis; and that Ethiopia could be of importance for U.S. air-routes to India and the Far East. The U.S. policy of nonrecognition of the fascist occupation had won lasting appreciation from Ethiopian officials and so created a highly favorable climate for the implementation of that policy. The most important step taken in that direction by the U.S. government was to grant lend-lease assistance to Ethiopia. That decision had been reached even before a request had been formulated by the Ethiopian government.

Given the political and commercial restrictions exercised by the British, it proved difficult for the U.S. government to assume the initiative.

---

[27] See Despatch No. 254, October 17, 1944, Amlegation, Addis Ababa, 741.8411/10-1744. For a cryptic reference to explicit British warning, see Despatch Amlegation No. 257, December 9, 1944, 741.8411/12-944. Also, see Memorandum Amembassy, London, April 14, 1944, 844.00/555; Despatch Amlegation, Addis Ababa, October 24, 1944, *For. Rels.*, 1944, Vol. V, 77; Memorandum, Department of State, November 24, 1944, 884.00/2444, and December 6, 1944, 865.014/12-644.

Indeed, the British objected to the granting of lend-lease assistance, and the opposition in economic and commercial matters made it difficult for Washington to take steps in such fields as currency, oil and mineral concessions, and airlines. Initiative in such matters almost inevitably fell to persons like the Governor of the State Bank of Ethiopia and the author, who, though Americans, were employees of the Ethiopian government without links to the U.S. government. These steps had to be taken piecemeal.

One modest step in the direction of freeing Ethiopia from the trammels of British currency controls, which were continually absorbing all the dollars produced by Ethiopian exports and sharply reducing imports from the United States, was taken in 1945 by the American Governor of the State Bank, Mr. Blowers. In that year the East African shilling was replaced by a new currency, the Ethiopian dollar. While that action did not free Ethiopia from the pound sterling, it laid the groundwork for eventually detaching it and basing it on the U.S. dollar—as was done in 1948 when the pound was devalued. This step was taken by the second Governor of the State Bank, also an American. However, even that first move would not have been possible without seeking and obtaining U.S. assistance in the form of a loan of five million ounces of silver for the minting of the divisional coinage, as well as assistance in the printing of the new paper currency. All of this was done at the U.S. Mint in Philadelphia. The United States showed that it was prepared to help, provided Ethiopia took the initiative.

Less assistance was forthcoming with respect to the railway from Addis Ababa to Djibouti. In the 1944 Agreement, the British consented to hand over to an administration designated by Ethiopia that portion of the railway (7/8ths) which lay within her borders. That single life-line carried all of Ethiopia's foreign commerce until the return of Eritrea in 1952. Foreseeing that the British would refuse to hand over the railway unless Ethiopia could assure proper management, contact was made with a reputable American engineering firm which had had experience in Ethiopia before the war and was *persona grata* to the British. A transport survey was conducted first, assisted in part by the efficient American Technical Mission to Ethiopia. However, just as the Ethiopian officials were on the point of signing a management agreement, the Department of State intervened by stating that such an agreement would prove embarrassing to the United States in its relations with the French. (It would be interesting to speculate what might have been the reaction had that question come up in 1967—when the French required removal of all U.S. NATO installations in France—instead of 1945.) In the end, the French recovered the administration of the entire line, despite the fact that they had forfeited their right in this respect, since they had violated the terms of the

concession by transporting Italian arms and munitions to Ethiopia.[28]
Another major problem was that of air transport. Under the 1942 agreement, only British airlines could operate into and out of Ethiopia, which meant that control and censorship of travel and communications remained in alien hands. The Department of State had already protested this unusually restrictive requirement, since it viewed Ethiopia as a possible strategic point in the development of American carrier (airline) networks through the Middle East and the Far East. However, here again, the United States was in no position to take the initiative. Consequently, when the Ethiopian delegation arrived in San Francisco in April 1945 for the conference to draft the UN Charter, the author asked the appropriate Department of State official which U.S. carrier had been certified by the United States to operate in the Cairo-Addis Ababa-Aden area. The response was TWA. Immediately contact was made with representatives of that company and, after many confidential discussions at which the Department of State was not represented, a management contract was concluded. The Ethiopian government put up all of the capital. Eventually the agreement became known to three very disgruntled sets of competitors—the British, the French and the Swedes.[29]

Once the project had been launched, the U.S. government provided invaluable assistance. Surplus DC-47s were made available from stocks parked at the edge of Payne Field outside Cairo, some planes were cannibalized in order to get others flying, and aviation dumps in the vicinity were picked over for supplies. Later, the Export-Import Bank made generous loans to permit the acquisition, first, of two Convairs, and later, of two DC-6s, a Constellation, five Boeing 727s, and finally two Boeing 707s. There were, of course, difficulties, particularly in personnel, which initially were not carefully chosen. These problems, along with the need for inventories of spare parts and establishment of maintenance centers, were eventually solved. Far more difficult were the severe obstacles interposed by the British to the development of a route structure, especially as the Ethiopian Airlines soon outperformed the British East African Airways to the point of pushing the latter toward bankruptcy. Before the recent revolution, Ethiopian Airlines, which by then was flying to five European capitals, to the West Coast of Africa, and to Shanghai, was a superb success story, accomplished without government subsidy. Now it is moribund.

---

[28] Article 7 of the Original Act of Concession of March 9, 1894, stated: "La compagnie ne pourra charger des troupes ou du matériel de guerre, pour les faire entrer ou sortir du pays, sans une lettre du Roi des Rois d'Ethiopie; si elle acceptait de tels transports sans un ordre, elle devrait abandonner le chemin de fer au Gouvernement d'Ethiopie." Text in Carlo Rossetti, *Storia diplomatica del'Etiopia* (Torino: Società Tipografico-Editrice Nazionale, 1910), p. 136.

[29] See Ralph Herrmanns, *Carl Gustav von Rosen* (Stockholm: Wahlström and Widstrand, 1975), pp. 162-163.

More important than all of these ventures, however, was finding a solution to the problem of the Ogaden, still under British occupation. The opening of air service to the territory by the Ethiopian Airlines established a link which the British were in no position to cut off. But Ethiopian presence in some other ostensible form was necessary.[30] An oil concession granted by the Ethiopian government would serve such a purpose. As in other matters of this nature, Washington was careful to keep its distance. In far-off wartime Ethiopia, no texts of other concession agreements were available. Consequently, the American Legation requested Washington to obtain some from the States, but none was supplied. Only by indirect means and after critical delays was it possible to lay hands on texts used in the industry. The negotiations were completed without the advice or assistance of the Department of State,[31] but once the concession was signed the Department began to be of help.

Problems with the British arose the instant the project was launched in the field. These were of three types: (1) The British insisted that no company trucks, materials, drilling equipment or personnel could move directly into the Ogaden, but had to pass first through British Somaliland, even though this meant a doubling back detour. All vehicles registered in Ethiopia had to be re-registered there. A 1.5 per cent tax on the value of the vehicles and equipment was levied and had to be paid in advance, and a large deposit had to be made on each piece of equipment as a guarantee that it would not be left in the Ogaden. Applications to the British authorities for prospecting permits had to be renewed every three months.

(2) Another problem was resistance by local tribesmen to the presence of drilling crews. According to company reports, outbreaks appeared to coincide with the arrival in drilling areas of British authorities, who asserted that they could not assume responsibility for restoring order. The problem became so severe that at one point the company temporarily withdrew its personnel from the area and proposed canceling the concession.

(3) A third problem grew out of the reservation on subterranean water appended to the 1944 agreement. Under this clause, the British were in a position to prevent the sinking of water wells preliminary to exploratory drilling for oil. This difficulty was eventually resolved, and the delight of

---

[30] The 1944 Agreement required the flying of the Ethiopian flag at every location where the British flag was flown. As a result, no flags were flown in the Ogaden. However, in a joint speech by the Chief Administrator and the Military Governor to representatives of the local tribes (Isaak and Septs), the British government was careful to set out the exact legal position of British occupation of the Ogaden in a strictly objective fashion. Rodd, p. 489.

[31] Except for one procedural recommendation by the U.S. Minister. Despatch, Amlegation, Addis Ababa, September 22, 1944, 884.6363/9-2244.

the local inhabitants at having new sources of water forced the hands of the authorities and brought to an end the resistance of tribesmen to the presence of drilling crews.

It was only in the latter half of 1948, three years after the signing of the concession, that operations finally got under way. This breakthrough resulted from the conclusion of an agreement on July 24 by which the British undertook to withdraw from the Ogaden, with the exception of fringe areas along the frontiers with Italian and British Somalilands. That such an agreement was concluded at all was due less to the constant pressure by Ethiopia and occasional pressure by the U.S. Embassy, than to broad developments in international diplomacy and, more specifically, the conflicts and rivalries among the four great powers concerning the future of the three former Italian colonies in Africa.

The Problems of the Ogaden and Eritrea, 1948-1952

The foreign ministers of the four great powers and their deputies had been meeting late in 1945 and in 1946 in preparation for the Paris Peace Conference to be convened in July 1946. The fate of the three Italian colonies (Libya, Eritrea and Somaliland) in Africa figured largely in these discussions. The British project for a Greater Somaliland met with a cool reception. The Soviet Union was opposed for two reasons. It foresaw the eventual construction of a British base at the mouth of the Red Sea and the entrance to the Indian Ocean, which would be immune from attack through the Middle East, unlike the base at Aden. Moreover, such a scheme included Italian Somaliland, one of the three colonies under discussion. As early as the Potsdam Conference in 1945, the Soviet Union had demanded at least one of these colonies, preferably Libya.[32] This demand outraged Prime Minister Clement Atlee, particularly since Libya had been the battlefield of Marshal Montgomery's victories, to which the Soviet Union had made no contribution and since the British had already established a military base in the eastern province of Cyrenaica.

The Soviets were rebuffed on Libya. The Greater Somaliland formula, consequently, appeared to the Soviet Union as a device for assuring that the British would obtain at least two of the three colonies. France had even more to lose by that formula since it included French Somaliland as well. As already indicated, the Department of State had previously communicated to the British its concern about the Greater Somaliland project, at least insofar as it involved the Ogaden, arguing that loss of the Ogaden in

---

[32] James R. Byrnes, *Speaking Frankly* (New York: Harper & Brothers, 1947), pp. 76, 95.

order to obtain Eritrea would be too high a price for Ethiopia to pay. It would lead to disorders and would amount to a surrender by the United Nations of the territory the League of Nations had betrayed in 1936. The Department of State added that cession of the Ogaden to Greater Somaliland would logically lead to the cession of French Somaliland, which the French would never accept, and finally, that loss of the Ogaden would jeopardize the Sinclair Oil concession.[33]

This broad opposition placed the British government under pressure to modify the Greater Somaliland formula so as to blunt some of the criticism. Yet a retreat under pressure ran the risk of becoming a renunciation. Accordingly, a public declaration was decided upon. This was made by Foreign Secretary Ernest Bevin in the House of Commons on June 4, 1946, just before the convening of the Paris Peace Conference.[34] In that declaration, French Somaliland was dropped, and there was an indication that Britain would not insist on including Italian Somaliland in the project.

That move did not, however, resolve the deadlock which persisted throughout the Paris Conference. The peace treaty with Italy, therefore, left the question to be determined by the four great powers (Article 23), but with the added proviso that if no solution was reached by the fall of 1948, the whole problem would be taken to the UN General Assembly. In the interim, the foreign ministers' deputies continued their discussions.

At their 1947 talks in London, the Soviet Deputy Foreign Minister made a particular point of asking the Ethiopian representative whether it was true that Ethiopia was disposed to give up the Ogaden in order to gain British support for the return of Eritrea.[35] The answer was "No."

By the latter half of 1948, not only had no solution been reached by the four great powers, but presidential elections in the United States and nationwide elections in Italy were in the offing. The United States accordingly favored the return to Italy of Somaliland, in order to court the ethnic vote in the presidential elections and forestall a communist victory in the Italian elections. The Soviet Union by this time was also in favor of returning the former colony to Italy for precisely the opposite reason, that of promoting a communist victory in the Italian elections. France had an entirely different motive for seeking the return of Somaliland to Italy. She was the resolute defender of the status quo ante for all three former

---

[33] Memoranda, Department of State, June 5, 1946, 865.014/6-546, and October 21, 1946, 865.014/10-2146. See also Despatch No. 110, May 11, 1946, Amlegation, Addis Ababa, 884.014/5-1146, and No. 149, June 20, 1946, 884.014/16-2046.

[34] *Parliamentary Debates*, House of Commons, June 4, 1946, Vol. 423, cols. 1840-1841.

[35] Despatches, Italian Colonies, Nos. 90,91, November 13, 19, 1947, Amembassy, London, 865.014/11-1247 and -1847. Memorandum, Department of State, November 21, 1947, 884.014/11-2147; cf. also 865.014/6-1747.

colonies, lest a change in the status of Libya threaten French rule in adjoining Tunisia.

Under these circumstances the British government did not relish the prospect of debates at the General Assembly where the Soviet delegate would air in public the question asked of, and the answer given by, the Ethiopian representative at the closed hearings in London the previous year. Moreover, few in the General Assembly would appreciate why the British had to hold on to a territory which Ethiopia had "lent" as a contribution toward the winning of a war that was ended three years ago. Not only had it become impolitic to insist upon its retention, but if the Ogaden were to become the price of British support for the return of Eritrea to Ethiopia, London would have to come up with some cover story to rationalize such a proposal. The British thus agreed on July 24, 1948, to return most of the Ogaden to Ethiopia, and the Sinclair Oil explorations then proceeded without a hitch.

This was a step forward in Ethiopia's strategy at the General Assembly to obtain the return of Eritrea without sacrificing the Ogaden. Attention was now turned to securing the return of the oldest portion of Ethiopia, Eritrea, a matter related to the problem of Greater Somaliland. Since 1924, Haile Sellassie had sought assistance from Italy, France and Britain in his effort to obtain access to the sea by a corridor or corridors under Ethiopian sovereignty. The ports that could have served Ethiopia were Massawa and Assab in Eritrea, Djibouti in French Somaliland, and Zeila and Berbera in British Somaliland, but all attempts were rebuffed up to the outbreak of the Italo-Ethiopian War.[36] That war was lost in large part because France, in pursuit of the policy of Stresa, had closed the port of Djibouti to the passage of arms by rail to Ethiopia.

The postwar Greater Somaliland project was a threat to consolidate foreign control over all but the Eritrean ports. Furthermore, since it was from Eritrea that Italy had launched its main invasion in 1935, considerations of national security had become dominant in Ethiopia's quest for the return of Eritrea. But these arguments were insufficient by themselves to convince other governments. Other arguments would have to be used—and, fortunately, were available. In many ways—for example, the Christianity of the highlands and the Moslem and animist predominance in the lowlands—Eritrea replicated the demographic, linguistic and cultural patterns of the rest of Ethiopia. Moreover, apart from Italian government subsidies, Eritrea had remained largely dependent on foodstuffs from northern Ethiopia, its soil and rainfall being less favorable

[36] Haile Sellassie I, *The Autobiography of Emperor Haile Sellassie I: My Life and Ethiopia's Progress 1892-1937*, translated and annotated by Edward Ullendorff (New York: Oxford University Press, 1976), pp. 93, 100, 102, 108, 146.

than those of adjoining Tigre. It was, consequently, scarcely surprising that the new four-power Commission of Investigation of the Former Italian Colonies found that a majority of the population (71 per cent in the highlands and about 30 per cent in the lowlands) appeared to favor a return to Ethiopia.[37]

In 1948 Britain still had Eritrea under military occupation, and it was clear that, without its support, Ethiopia could never obtain the return of that territory. The record of the next several years shows that, had it not been for the steadfast support of the British government, Ethiopia would never have obtained any satisfaction from the United Nations. Moreover, at no time during the United Nations debates did the British ever seek to exploit a quid pro quo. The United States played a helpful but somewhat more subordinate role. Washington remained sensitive to the domestic Italian vote and, therefore, proposed only token access to the sea for Ethiopia through Assab, whereas the British government urged the return of all the territory, except for the Western Province, which it hoped to annex to the Sudan. Italy's demand that Eritrea be returned to her was strongly supported by the large Latin American bloc, which consequently opposed Ethiopia's claim.[38] An even greater obstacle to the return of Eritrea, with its substantial Moslem minority, to the Christian government of Ethiopia was the Moslem opposition headed by Pakistan.

At the fourth session of the General Assembly in the autumn of 1949, Islamic, Arab and Soviet bloc opposition to Eritrea's return to Ethiopia and firm Latin American support of the proposal for Eritrean independence, suddenly advanced by Italy, made an impasse inevitable.[39] In the hope of devising some solution, the General Assembly adopted on November 21, 1949, Resolution 289(IV)C establishing a new commission, composed of Burma, Guatemala, Norway, Pakistan and the Union of South Africa, to investigate the problem afresh.[40]

---

[37] Commission for the Investigation of the Former Italian Colonies, Volumes I-IV (London, 1948); G.K.N. Trevaskis, *Eritrea: A Colony in Transition, 1941-1952* (London: Oxford University Press, 1968), pp. 89 ff.; Zewde Gabre-Sellassie, *Eritrea and Ethiopia in the Context of the Red Sea and Africa*, unpublished study presented at the Woodrow Wilson International Center for Scholars, March 1976, pp. 76-83.

[38] General Assembly Official Records (hereafter cited as GAOR), Third Session, second part, 218th Meeting, May 17, 1949, p. 593. The Soviet bloc voted against the British proposal supporting Ethiopia, and, with Latin America, was responsible for its defeat in the General Assembly, since it did not wish to see any accretion of territory to the Sudan so long as it was known as the Anglo-Egyptian Sudan and remained under British administration.

[39] For a careful study of the UN proposals, see Benjamin Rivlin, *The United Nations and the Italian Colonies* (New York: Carnegie Endowment for International Peace, Case Histories, No. 1, 1950).

[40] The mandate of the Commission was to take into account "(a) The wishes and welfare of the inhabitants of Eritrea, including the views of the various racial, religious, and political groups of the provinces of the territory and the capacity of the people for self-government; (b) The interests of peace and security in East Africa; (c) The rights and claims of Ethiopia based on geographical, historical, ethnic or economic reasons, including in particular Ethiopia's legitimate need for adequate access to the sea...."

At this juncture popular support for a return of Eritrea to Ethiopia rather dramatically increased, due in large part to the *voltafaccia* on the part of Italy in favor of independence for the territory. Italian initiative and funds led to the creation of an independence bloc in Eritrea, consisting of all opponents of a return to Ethiopia, including various Italian and pro-Italian groups, the (Christian) Liberal Progressive Party, and the Moslem League of the Western Province.[41] However, the non-Italian elements soon came to fear an Italian-dominated independent state, and, in addition, the Liberal Progressive Party feared that in such a situation the Moslems would win out over the Christians.[42] The party's decision to join the Unionists was accelerated by acts of terrorism perpetrated by clandestine pro-Union elements. For their part, the Moslem League of the Western Province also feared that an independent Eritrea would not be economically viable, and in that case the province would be annexed by the Sudan and its inhabitants would fall under the domination of their traditional enemies, the Hadendowa.[43] Both the Moslems and the Christians came to the conclusion that they would enjoy greater autonomy in association with Ethiopia than in an independent state. Thus, the independence formula was defeated by popular opposition, and the five-member commission had to recognize that support for a return to Ethiopia was widespread.[44] It became difficult for the General Assembly to reject such a solution in one form or another.

In this situation, Latin American opposition to a formula of association with Ethiopia disappeared, but this was not the case with the Arab states. Factors other than demographic or purely religious considerations were at stake. Their concern at the appearance of a non-Moslem, non-Arab, Western-oriented state on the western shores of the Red Sea, for them an Arab lake, was translated into propaganda, money and arms for promoting secession. Confronted with this hostility, Ethiopia, the "interloper," did what might be expected under the circumstances: she drew closer to the other non-Moslem, non-Arab state at the northern end of the Red Sea—Israel.

With Latin American opposition at a minimum, the Italian elections out of the way, and only the Arab and Soviet opposition remaining, the United States was able to be of considerable assistance in devising the

[41] Trevaskis, p. 95; Patrick Gilkes, *The Dying Lion* (London: Julian Friedmann, 1975), p. 194.

[42] Trevaskis, p. 97; Christopher Clapham. *Ethiopia and Somalia* (London: International Institute for Strategic Studies, Adelphi Paper No. 93, 1972), p. 9.

[43] Trevaskis, pp. 69-97; P. M. Holt, *The Modern History of the Sudan* (New York: Grove Press, 1961), p. 11; *Report of the UN Commission for Eritrea*, GAOR, Supplement No. 5 (A/1285), Fifth Session, p. 19, para. 121; Rivlin, p. 38; UN Documents A/C.1/SR., nos. 269-272.

[44] *Report of the UN Commission for Eritrea*, GAOR, Fifth Session, Supplement No. 5 (A/1285), p. 21, para. 132; p. 26, para. 173; but see p. 31, paras. 204 and 205. Also see Trevaskis, pp. 98, 130.

formula for the federation of Eritrea and Ethiopia. This solution had been proposed by the five-power commission and was elaborated in UN Resolution 390V of December 2, 1950.[45] The two American lawyers advising the United States and Ethiopia in the new informal six-state drafting commission (United States, Britain, Italy, Mexico, Brazil and Ethiopia) easily reached agreement on the legal complexities involved, and U.S. constitutional concepts and phraseology entered directly into the language of the UN Resolution. The United States was also helpful in supporting Ethiopia's version of the boundary that should separate the Ogaden from former Italian Somaliland—but this problem remains unresolved today.

The Period of Collaboration, 1952-1960

Ethiopia was grateful to the United States for its support on the Eritrean and Ogaden issues in 1950 and, as a gesture of appreciation, became the one non-NATO state in the area to contribute a contingent to the UN forces in South Korea under U.S. command.

The U.S. defense installations in Ethiopia and the mutual defense agreements between the United States and Ethiopia grew out of the Eritrean discussions at the United Nations. The United States had indicated to the Ethiopian government, in advance of the December 1950 Resolution, that once Ethiopia re-assumed sovereignty over Eritrea, the United States would want to conclude an agreement by which U.S. personnel would take over the large communications center outside Asmara. Following the adoption of the UN Resolution, U.S. pressure became more noticeable and insistent.[46] Ethiopia did not fail to perceive in that situation the opportunity for a quid pro quo. For some time she had been pressing the United States for arms and a military mission, but Washington refused to listen so long as the British Military Mission remained in Ethiopia. However, in 1952 (the year Ethiopia re-assumed sovereignty over Eritrea), for reasons of its own, the British government declared that it could no longer continue to supply arms or a mission. The way then became clear for Ethiopia to develop the quid pro quo.

The United States wanted the communications base at Asmara (the base was subsequently named "Kagnew" in honor of the Ethiopian contin-

---

[45] GAOR, Fifth Session, Supplement No. 20 (A/1775), p. 20. See also the *Final Report* of the UN Commissioner on the Establishment of the Federation, GAOR, Seventh Session, Supplement No. 15 (A/2188) (1952).

[46] As early as 1948, Admiral William D. Leahy, Chairman of the Joint Chiefs of Staff, insisted that the United States must remain inflexible in its demand to retain the installation there. *For. Rels.*, 1948, Vol. III, 933-934.

gent in Korea) because it was located in the tropics far from the north and south magnetic poles, the aurora borealis and magnetic storms, in a zone where the limited degree of seasonal variations between sunrise and sunset reduced the need for numerous frequency changes. It was an important addition to the worldwide network of U.S. communications including the Philippines, Ethiopia, Morocco and Arlington, Virginia, and could also serve the NATO area within Western Europe whenever electrical and magnetic disturbances upset communications in those higher latitudes.[47] In other words, the base at Asmara had little to do with either Ethiopia or Africa.

Progress in negotiating the two related base and arms assistance agreements encountered heavy resistance in the Pentagon. Two factors broke the stalemate. One was timely concessions on the base agreement by the Ethiopian government. Responding to Pentagon insistence, Ethiopia agreed to a much longer-term lease—25 years—and to a much lower rental than those the United States was negotiating in base agreements with other countries at that time. In addition, Ethiopia reluctantly dropped her efforts to obtain a commitment from the United States to defend the base should the presence of U.S. military personnel make it a target for infiltration or attack from the socialist bloc or Arab states.

A second factor in breaking down Pentagon resistance to the agreements, especially the arms assistance agreement, was the use to which the Ethiopian government was able to put the "Northern Tier" concept being developed at that time by Secretary of State John Foster Dulles, which led to the Baghdad Pact. The negotiators for Ethiopia proposed that she should form part of a "Southern Tier" or secondary line of defense against communism in the Middle East. That type of argument facilitated the finding by the Secretaries of State and Defense that the defense of Ethiopia was essential to the defense of the free world. However, subsequent events made it clear that had there not been an urgent need for a worldwide communications base in Eritrea, there would have been no arms assistance agreement with Ethiopia.[48]

Following the conclusion of the agreements, relations between the United States and Ethiopia developed along classic lines. Ethiopia profited enormously from arms aid, the MAAG mission, and the rentals and expenditures produced by the base agreement. The Emperor's first visit

---

[47] U.S. Congress, House, Committee on Foreign Relations, *U.S. Policy and Request for Sale of Arms to Ethiopia*, Hearings before the Subcommittee on International Political and Military Affairs, 94th Cong., 1st sess., March 5, 1975 (Washington: GPO, 1975), p. 12.

[48] See the testimony of former Ambassador Edward Korry in U.S. Congress, Senate, Committee on Foreign Relations, *Ethiopia and the Horn of Africa*, Hearings before the Subcommittee on African Affairs, 94th Cong., 2nd sess., August 4, 1976 (Washington: GPO, 1976), p. 36.

to the United States took place the following year.[49] Ethiopia voted consistently with the United States at the UN General Assembly. By 1970 she had become the foremost recipient of U.S. military aid in all of Africa, apart from South Africa.[50]

It is beyond the scope of this study to enter into the confrontations between the United States and Egypt in 1956 which ended in Nasser's seizure of the Suez Canal. What is significant here is that, as a result, Arab xenophobia reached a point of frenzy. At the first London Conference on the Suez, a five-power commission, comprising the United States, Australia, Sweden, Iran and Ethiopia, was formed at the initiative of Secretary Dulles to proceed to Cairo for the purpose of persuading Nasser to abandon his plan to nationalize the canal in favor of an international regime.[51] Ethiopia was selected along with Iran to represent, as it were, partners in a sort of "Northern Tier" group. By agreeing to accept a place on the commission, Ethiopia took the risk of offending what was then the most powerful of the Arab states, but did so on the calculation that this was an acceptable price to pay for closer association with the United States.

She reached that decision also partly because Egypt at that time was leading the Arab attack on Ethiopia for having obtained Eritrea at the United Nations, and was beaming propaganda broadcasts to the Eritrean population urging secession. Cairo was also supporting its own version of the Greater Somaliland Movement, calling for the "Unity of the Valley of the Nile" under Egyptian leadership, and was actively pursuing that objective through its representative on the UN Advisory Commission to the Italian Trusteeship Administration in Somalia.

Nasser firmly rejected the proposals of the five-power commission. That action in itself was enough to cause deep concern as to the price Ethiopia might eventually have to pay for having joined others in pressing Nasser to accept proposals which he found offensive. That concern was, however, as nothing compared to the consternation that followed when Dulles suddenly executed an about-face, in substance accepting Nasser's position and abandoning Ethiopia to the wrath of her northern neighbor.

---

[49] Secretary Dulles had opposed the trip and, as it turned out, with good reason. After arriving in Washington, the Emperor suddenly decided to utilize the occasion for seeking, without previous preparation or notice, new measures of military and technical aid.

[50] U.S. military assistance to Ethiopia exceeded that supplied to other African states for three reasons: (1) other states gained independence only long after the 1953 program had been started; (2) Ethiopia had no precolonial relationship, so the United States was her primary supplier, whereas the former colonial powers continued to furnish arms to their erstwhile colonies; (3) military assistance was the quid pro quo for the continued presence of the U.S. defense installation in Eritrea. See the testimony of Assistant Secretary of State David D. Newsom in U.S. Congress, Senate, Committee on Foreign Relations, *U.S. Security Agreements and Commitments Abroad: Part 8, Ethiopia*, Hearings before the Subcommittee on U.S. Security Agreements and Commitments Abroad, 91st Cong., 2nd sess., June 1, 1970 (Washington, D.C.: GPO, 1970), p. 1952.

[51] See Herbert Finer, *Dulles Over Suez* (Chicago, Ill.: Quadrangle Books, 1964), pp. 48, 173-175.

Ethiopia's relations with Egypt quite naturally worsened, and the assassination in Mogadiscio in June 1957 of the Egyptian member of the UN Advisory Commission was laid at Ethiopia's doorstep. As for relations with the United States, the Dulles initiatives were damaging. The Richards Mission of 1957, followed by the Draper Mission in 1958 to develop support in the Middle East for the Eisenhower Doctrine,[52] were not only failures but contributed to a further deterioration in relations.

The year 1959 marked an event of considerable significance in the evolution of U.S.-Ethiopian relations. Ethiopian opposition to any U.S. support for the emerging state of Somalia posed a dilemma for Washington in 1959, on the eve of independence for the British and former Italian Somalilands, fixed for 1960. To the U.S. government, a political formula of British origin seemed to offer a palliative if not a solution. Neither of the two Somalilands was capable of existing without massive infusions of foreign aid. Perhaps the union of the two territories might alleviate some of the asperities of independence. That was the approach the British proposed to the United States. The latter, in its frustration, found the British formula seductive, but apparently failed to take into consideration the fact that Britain had long proposed the union of the two territories as part of its own Greater Somaliland project.

In late January 1959, following talks with the British, the U.S. Embassy, in a written communication to the Ethiopian government, indicated that it supported the British proposal for the union of the British and former Italian Somalilands. Such a formula had been broached orally by the British in London and Addis Ababa in talks with Ethiopian officials. The U.S. written notification of support was doubly damaging to relations. Whereas the British had astutely limited their approach to the Ethiopians by keeping it on the elusive basis of oral exchanges, the U.S. move was in black and white. Far worse, only after delivery of the American note did the British go public with a formal proposal by Colonial Secretary Lennox Boyd,[53] and thereby "burned their bridges behind them." Ethiopia, now convinced that the United States was ganging up on her with the British to revive the hated Greater Somaliland project, reacted with indignation. The Emperor hied himself off to Moscow.

The Ethiopian reaction was also unfortunate. In the first place, relations with Moscow had been distant because of Soviet opposition to Ethiopia on the Eritrean question at the General Assembly. The essential point, however, was that the traditionally successful policy of playing off one side against the other could not work very well in the case of the

---

[52] Eisenhower's Message to Congress, January 5, 1957, in Department of State, *United States Policy in the Middle East, September 1956-June 1957: Documents* (Washington, D.C.: GPO, 1957), pp. 15-23.

[53] *New York Times*, February 10, 11, 1959.

United States, which operated under the inhibitions of the Monroe and NATO doctrines. Ethiopia was able to obtain arms assistance from the United States essentially because of the latter's need for a global communications base in Eritrea, whereas the British proposal for the union of two Somali territories directly involved the NATO doctrine in Africa. The trip to Moscow did, however, produce slight dividends in the form of an opening of a four hundred million ruble credit and the subsequent negotiation of an expanded arms assistance agreement with the United States in 1960.

The situation in 1959 reflected a downtrend in U.S.-Ethiopian relations resulting from sudden reversals by Secretary of State Dulles in regard to the Suez and Greater Somaliland issues, thereby exposing Ethiopia to the full blast of Arab hostility. Adding to the difficulty of maintaining a pro-Western stance were the mounting pressures from three conferences of nonaligned states: Bandung in 1955, the All-African People's in 1958, and the Asian-African People's Solidarity Organization in 1959. Repeated warnings, including those of the author in his capacity as foreign affairs adviser, accomplished little in halting the drift of Ethiopia toward the Soviet Union under pressures from the nonaligned camp.

3.
The Greater Somaliland Problem and the Djibouti Territory, 1960-1977

THE JOINT Anglo-American *démarche* of 1959 for the union of the British and the former Italian Somalilands acted as a signal to the Greater Somaliland forces in Somalia to issue on August 30, 1959, what became known as the "Mogadiscio Manifesto."[54] This was a call for the creation of a Greater Somaliland to include parts of Kenya and Ethiopia, and all of British and French Somalilands. At the same time, in Oslo at UN-sponsored negotiations, under the chairmanship of Trygve Lie, concerning the boundary between Ethiopia and Somalia, the spokesman for Somalia called for application of past Anglo-Italian and Anglo-French-Italian agreements partitioning Ethiopia into colonial spheres of influence.[55] Such treaties would have allocated all of the Ogaden to Somalia.

Yet, it should be noted that the Mogadiscio Manifesto in fact departed from its alleged ethnic base to cast its net far wider than the British Greater Somaliland proposals. It laid claim to the pasturelands and rivers of the Galla-dominated Sidamo and Bale provinces of Ethiopia, clearly no part of the Ogaden, and to the Afar people who live not only in French Somaliland but in northeastern Ethiopia as well. Both the Afars and the Issas extend far into Ethiopia—approximately 60 per cent of the Issas and 80 per cent of the Afars live there. Most of the tribal leaders, including the Ougaz of the Issas and the Sultan of Aussa (Afars), reside in Ethiopia.[56] (The Sultan of Aussa fled from the Derg in June 1975, first to Djibouti and then into exile in Saudi Arabia.) The Issas are rivals of the Gaddabursi inhabiting former British Somaliland and Ethiopia. The Afars occupy the Red Sea coast as far north as Marsa Fatma, some 100 miles south of Massawa. Yet the Afars are not Somalis and are rivals of the Issas. The Djibouti territory, therefore, serves as the

---

[54] See *The Somaliland News* (British Somaliland), September 7, 1959, Issue No. 32, p. 1, dateline August 30, 1959, from Mogadiscio (Somalia), which reported on the convening in Mogadiscio of the conference at which the Pan Somali National Movement (Greater Somaliland) was established. The Prime Minister, Abdullahi Issa, long-time head of the Somali Youth League, and other ministers were present. Yusuf Ismail Samater was elected secretary of a preparatory committee to arrange for the First Congress of the Movement.

[55] GAOR, Twelfth Session, Supplement No. 18 (A/3805), p. 30; Thirteenth Session, Supplement No. 18 (A/4090), p. 37; Fourteenth Session (A/4325).

[56] Virginia Thompson and Richard Adloff, *Djibouti and the Horn of Africa* (Stanford, Calif.: Stanford University Press, 1968), pp. 36, 108; Philippe Oberlé, *Afars et Somalis* (Paris: Presence Africaine, 1971), pp. 38-43; Lewis, *A Pastoral Democracy*, pp. 36-42. For the revolt of the Afars in the Ethiopian province adjoining the Territory of the Afars and the Issas, see *Le Monde*, September 21, 1974; *Africa Confidential*, December 5, 1975, p. 2; René Bénezra, "Le Territoire Français des Afars et des Issas," *Afrique Contemporaine*, July-August 1975, pp. 20, 23.

gateway to a wide expansion of the Greater Somaliland Movement to the north, by its claim to the Afars, an ethnic group opposed to association with the Somalis.

The Djibouti territory thus became the target of Somalia's propaganda and diplomatic efforts immediately following attainment of independence in 1960.[57] Simultaneously, Somalia supported and directed the PMP (Parti du Mouvement Populaire) in Djibouti, later replaced by the LPAI (African People's League for Independence), which was led by Hassan Gouled and was in the pay of Mogadiscio.[58] (Following independence in 1977, Hassan Gouled was elected President of Djibouti by the majority pro-Somali party, the Popular Union for Independence.) The PMP and its successor were also assisted by the FLCS (Front for the Liberation of the Somali Coast), based in Mogadiscio and Baghdad.[59] In 1976, in pursuit of the Somali objective, President Siad Barre made a trip to Paris in order to bring pressure on President Giscard d'Estaing, but apparently to no avail. Reacting to the Somali campaign, Ethiopia has supported the movement for union of the territory with Ethiopia by various means, including a speech by the Emperor and setting up the organization, Mouvement pour la Libération du Territoire de Djibouti (MLD).[60]

Until recently, France was glad to abide by Ethiopia's desire that the French remain in Djibouti as a means of obstructing the Somali campaign to incorporate that territory in a Greater Somaliland. The French presence there has also served U.S. and British interests, for they do not wish to see the key port of Djibouti fall under the control of a Soviet-dominated Somalia. But throughout the early 1970s France found her position increasingly difficult to maintain with no less than eight Francophone states of Africa, along with OAU and UN resolutions, calling for her withdrawal.[61] As the only remaining colonial power in Africa and

---

[57] GAOR, Fifteenth Session, 945th Meeting, December 13, 1960, p. 1248. See also Somalia Ministry of Foreign Affairs, Public Relations Section, *The Somali Republic and the Organization of African Unity*, Mogadiscio, p. 25. At the Paris Peace Conference in 1918, Italy had already laid claim to the Djibouti Territory in a Memorandum of the Foreign Minister, Baron Sidney Sonnino, to Lord Balfour, October 30, 1918, text published in Francesco Salata, *Il Nodo di Gibuti, Storia Diplomatica su Documenti inediti Instituto per gli Studi di politica internazionale* (Milan, 1939), p. 277, also pp. 37, 47, 134, 273, 283-286, 307-310.

[58] Thompson and Adloff, p. 79; *Le Monde (Sélection hebdomadaire)*, August 25-31, 1966; *Africa Confidential*, August 6, 1976. See also I. M. Lewis, "Prospects in the Horn of Africa," *Africa Report*, April 1967, p. 37. On Hassan Gouled, see Oberlé, p. 243; *Le Monde*, February 14, 1976; *Africa Confidential*, May 13, 1977; *Washington Post*, June 27, 1977, p. A-1.

[59] Touval, pp. 144, 226; Thompson and Adloff, p. 84; Oberlé, p. 222. The recent kidnaping of the French Ambassador in Mogadiscio was the work of the Front for the Liberation of the Somali Coast. *Africa Research Bulletin: Political, Social and Cultural Series (ARB)*, 1975, p. 3565; *Africa Confidential*, January 24, 1975, p. 8; June 14, 1975, p. 7; and April 16, 1976, p. 7.

[60] Thompson and Adloff, pp. 110, 116, 124; *Le Monde (Sélection hebdomadaire)*, October 13-19, 1966.

[61] Senegal, Niger, Dahomey, Upper Volta, Togo, Gabon, Rwanda and Burundi were the eight states. At its 24th session in January 1975, the OAU Liberation Committee demanded decolonization of the Territory. *ARB*, 1975, p. 3483C.

herself in hostage to the Arab world with her twelve-year oil pact, France knew her departure was inevitable.

The ultimate blow to the French position was, however, delivered by Ethiopia herself. By 1975, the Syrian, Iraq and Libyan interventions in Eritrea had become so intense and the fighting so bitter that the Derg sought to buy time by bargaining away Djibouti. This was accomplished by the Derg's endorsement of the resolution adopted at the 1974 Rabat Conference of the Arab League calling for the independence of the territory.[62] Such a move surely was made out of desperation, since the obvious interest of the territory, once independent, would be to promote the independence of Eritrea. Ethiopia could thereby be deprived of access to the sea and be obliged to funnel all of her foreign trade through Djibouti. Moreover, such a solution obviously constituted a dangerous precedent for the Ogaden.

France found herself in these circumstances with scant opportunity for maneuver. Under pressure from Somalia and from Arab League members, she dumped her long-time protégé, Prime Minister Ali Aref Bourhan, an Afar, and replaced him with Abdallah Mohammed Kamil, in a government of national unity in which the Mogadiscio-controlled LPAI participates. The former prime minister, as reported in *Le Monde* (May 26, 1976), summed up the situation in Djibouti as follows: "Somalia 'calls the tune' in Djibouti just as the Soviet Union has 'called the tune' in Warsaw." ("L'ordre somalien régne à Djibouti comme ordre soviétique a régné à Varsovie.") At the OAU meeting in Port Louis, Mauritius, in June 1976, Somalia, in a thirteen-hour filibuster, opposed the attempts by Ethiopia and other states to require all members to guarantee the independence of the future state. The resolution was eventually adopted, but with a reservation on the part of Somalia.[63]

Djibouti, a broiling desert territory and port city on the Gulf of Aden, became independent on June 27, 1977. On that date, France and Djibouti signed an agreement under which France will station 4,000 troops in the new state. Although details of the pact are not yet available, the French troops will presumably provide temporary security for Djibouti. But the new state's major difficulties will be economic. It is heavily dependent on the railway to Ethiopia, which has traditionally produced over 80 per cent of Djibouti's revenue, thanks to the high freight rates set by the

---

[62] At the nonaligned conference in Sri Lanka in 1976, General Teferi Bante, chief delegate of Ethiopia, reaffirmed that position, declaring: "l'Ethiopie proclame sans équivoque que ni aujourd'hui ni dans le futur elle ne revendique tout ou partie du territoire de Djibouti indépendant. . . . L'Ethiopie non seulement soutient l'indépendance de Djibouti, mais elle pense que celle-ci est compatible avec ses intérêts nationaux." *Le Monde*, August 18, 1976.

[63] *New York Times*, June 30 and July 12, 1976. See also the *Washington Post*, February 21 and July 1, 1976; *U.S. News and World Report*, February 23, 1976, p. 38. For a qualified reversal by President Siad Barre on January 7, 1977, see *Le Monde*, January 6, 1977.

French.[64] Despite these exorbitant charges, the French claim that the railway has been operating at a deficit, due largely to Ethiopia's increasing use of the Eritrean ports of Assab and Massawa.

Thus, independent Djibouti will no doubt find itself in a financial bind, unless friendly states come to its aid—and this probably means a "bail-out" by Somalia and the Soviet Union, and eventual annexation by Somalia. The pro-Somali President and National Assembly seem disposed to "request" annexation, not least because during the summer of 1977 Somali "irregulars" operating in the Ogaden against Ethiopian forces cut the rail line between Addis Ababa and Djibouti at several points. Since the French troops in Djibouti are not likely to resist annexation, we will no doubt soon witness another step forward in the creation of a Greater Somaliland.

Thus, the basic problem for Ethiopia has been Arab support for a Greater Somaliland which, under the leadership of Syria and later Libya, grew steadily stronger over the years. For example, at the World Islamic Congress convened in Mogadiscio in December 1964, the Syrian representative called for the support of all Moslems for the Greater Somaliland Movement. At the OAU summit conference at Addis Ababa in 1973, Libya proclaimed Ethiopia to be an imperialist state faithless to African traditions, because of her opposition to the aspirations of the Somalis for a Greater Somaliland, and called for the removal of OAU headquarters from Addis Ababa.[65] At the end of 1973 Somalia became a member of the Arab League.

---

[64] In addition, through its public corporation, the *Compagnie de l'Afrique orientale*, France levied astronomically high porthandling charges and inspection and statistical fees. For example, it cost the Ethiopian Airlines less to on-load and ship an aircraft engine by sea from San Francisco 12,000 miles to Djibouti than it did to off-load it there and forward it by rail 600 miles to Addis Ababa. In 1949 the French government established the Djibouti franc, based on dollar deposits in New York banks. By that device, it was able to require Ethiopian shippers and importers to pay in U.S. dollars, rather than in Ethiopian dollars or French francs, for all rail transport charges in Ethiopia and all rail, statistical, inspection, handling and loading charges in Djibouti. Thus, France thoroughly exploited its control of Ethiopia's major access to the sea.

[65] *ARB*, May 1973, p. 2849A; *Africa Confidential*, November 2, 1973, p. 3; B. N. Degorge, "Le facteur islamique dans le conflit erythréen," *Revue française d'études politiques africaines*, May 1975, p. 77.

4.
Eritrea: From Federation to Secession, 1952-1977

ARAB HOSTILITY toward Ethiopia, however, has been concentrated chiefly against her control over Eritrea, ever since the UN allocated that territory to Ethiopia, thereby threatening the Arabs' monopoly of the southern reaches of the Red Sea and their objective of transforming it into an Arab lake. From the Arab point of view, the best way to remove that threat would be to promote the secession and independence of Eritrea.

Leadership of this Arab effort was first exercised by Egypt through radio propaganda, calling for Eritrean independence, addressed as much to Christians as to Moslems. Subsequently, following Egypt's detente with Ethiopia,[66] the initiative passed to Syria and other radical Arab states: Libya, Iraq, and the People's Democratic Republic of Yemen (South Yemen), with sporadic support in lesser measure from Lebanon, Saudi Arabia, the Yemen Arab Republic (North Yemen) and Egypt.[67] The instrument for achieving the objective of independence was the Eritrean Liberation Front (ELF) established in Cairo in 1961. Noting the increasingly organized nature of the movement, the Ethiopian government in 1962 ill-advisedly proclaimed the end of the federation established by UN Resolution 390V and the re-integration of Eritrea.[68] Clearly, these for-

---

[66] Improvement of relations was due largely to the ability of Haile Sellassie to develop a close personal friendship with Nasser and later with Sadat. This relationship was nurtured in part by the fact that for 1,500 years the Patriarch of Alexandria had presided over the Coptic Church of Ethiopia, whose communicants vastly outnumbered the politically important Copt minority in Egypt. Moreover, Egypt has always been mindful of the fact that Ethiopia, with Eritrea, supplies nearly 84 per cent of the waters of the Nile in Egypt.

[67] For a concise account of the radical Arab leadership of the Eritrean independence movement, see M. Abir, "The Contentious Horn of Africa," *Conflict Studies*, June 1972; *Africa Report*, March-April 1975, pp. 14-17. Kuwait, despite its highly conservative orientation, has been a large supplier of (Soviet) arms. *Africa Confidential*, April 11, 1975, p. 7.

See also the statement by George W. Bader of the Department of Defense, in U.S. Congress, House, Committee on Foreign Affairs, *U.S. Policy and Request for Sale of Arms to Ethiopia*, Hearings before the Subcommittee on International Political and Military Affairs, 94th Cong., 1st sess., March 5, 1975 (Washington, D.C.: GPO, 1975), p. 10.

[68] While deploring this action, both ethically and politically, the author must observe that it was not entirely without legal basis. Both the American and British members of the informal six-state drafting committee (see above, p. 22) had particularly stressed to the Ethiopian Foreign Minister that acceptance by Ethiopia of the provision in the Federal Act (paragraph 13 of UN Resolution 390A V) requiring its adoption by the Eritrean Assembly would thereby justify termination of the Federation upon a concurring vote of that Assembly, without need of approval by the UN General Assembly. In fact, in previous years, the Eritrean Assembly had voted resolutions similar to that adopted in 1962, which the Ethiopian government had refrained from invoking. It might also be observed that the federations of Libya and the Cameroon, both envisaged by UN resolutions, were similarly dissolved without recourse to ratification by the UN General Assembly. Finally, according to paragraph 3 of Annex XI to the Treaty of Peace with Italy (1947), Cmd 7481, p. 92, once the General Assembly had made its recommendation to the four powers, its role was terminated. It was these powers that had the final responsibility.

eign influences would not have taken hold so readily had the Ethiopian government not been guilty of egregious errors on its part. For example, it sought from the outset to insist on the use of the Amharic language for government communications rather than the Tigrinya, although the two are closely related. It proceeded to the appointment of subservient Eritreans in federal posts and the awarding to compliant bidders of federal contracts in Eritrea.[69] On the other hand, it should be recognized that Eritreans profited immensely from their appointments and business opportunities in Ethiopia as a result of the federation. Fully one-third of the Ethiopian army, nearly one-half of her air force and police, and a large but undetermined portion of her business community have been Eritrean.[70] It is this influential interest group that views with concern the possible secession of Eritrea.

The consequence of this re-integration of Eritrea in 1962 was a redoubling of efforts by the Arab states, through propaganda, money and arms, to undermine that union. Syria moved to the forefront in providing headquarters for the ELF, and supplying its Christian leader, Tedla Bairu, former head of the Unionists, with a monthly stipend of 3,000 Syrian pounds, until his removal.[71] Anti-Syrian demonstrations took place in Ethiopia, and relations were broken off with Iraq because of the latter's support of the ELF. Over time, three secessionist groups have emerged: the Eritrean Liberation Front, largely Pan-Arab in orientation; the Eritrean People's Liberation Front (EPLF), largely Marxist in outlook; and the ELF-PLF (Popular Forces for the Liberation of Eritrea), under Osman Saleh Sabbe, former ELF leader, with substantial Arab funds at his disposal. The ELF and the EPLF eventually agreed to combine their operations, leaving the ELF-PLF movement outside and concentrating its efforts more on the eastern highlands and coastal areas.[72] Violence, organized by the ELF and the PLF, became endemic. At the 1975 Kampala OAU summit conference, Tunisia proposed that the ELF delegation be given official observer status, whereupon Ethiopia broke off diplomatic relations with Tunisia.[73]

---

[69] Gilkes, p. 195; Robert L. Hess, *Ethiopia: The Modernization of Autocracy* (Ithaca, N.Y.: Cornell University Press, 1970), pp. 184-185; Clapham, pp. 9ff.

[70] See the statement by Bader, in U.S. Congress, House, *U.S. Policy and Request for Sale of Arms to Ethiopia*, p. 14: "Traditionally the Eritreans have provided a disproportionate amount of the middle class in Ethiopia as to the technicians, bureaucrats, and private businessmen and that is true in Addis Ababa as well as elsewhere in the country."

[71] *Africa Confidential*, December 19, 1974, p. 3; Abir, p. 3; Gilkes, pp. 196-199.

[72] *Africa Confidential*, December 19, 1974, p. 3; February 7, 1975, p. 8; October 24, 1975, p. 6; May 28, 1976, p. 6.

[73] *Africa*, September 1975, p. 74. On the violence in Eritrea, see J. Bowyer Bell, Jr., "Endemic Insurgency and International Order: The Eritrean Experience," *Orbis*, Summer 1975.

The Seven-Day (1967) and Yom Kippur (1973) wars reminded the Arab states of the strategic importance of Ethiopia's presence at and above the Strait of Bab el Mandeb. For some time before the 1973 conflict, the Arab world was aroused over persistent rumors that Ethiopia had granted Israel bases on her islands north of the entrance to the strait. In fact, the Ethiopian Foreign Minister who, in January 1973, undertook a tour of the North African states in the hope of persuading them to desist from their campaign in support of a Greater Somaliland, found that the officials were unwilling to discuss any matter other than the alleged existence of Israeli bases on the islands. Vigorous denials apparently failed to convince the Arab states that no such arrangement had been entered into or was even contemplated,[74] nor could the Arab states be persuaded to cease their efforts to promote the Greater Somaliland project.

[74] By 1973 Israeli Phantom jets had established ascendancy over the Red Sea as far south as Eritrea. Opportunities for military cooperation, therefore, arose at that juncture. Ethiopia was particularly careful, however, to make clear to Bar Lev, the Israeli Chief of Staff, during his visit to Addis Ababa in 1971, that any military cooperation or even an understanding was out of the question.

5.
Turmoil in the Horn of Africa, 1973-1977

THE YEAR 1973 marked an upsurge of Arab influence in the Horn and adjoining areas. The assassination in March of the U.S. Ambassador and his Counselor of Embassy in Khartoum, the Yom Kippur War in October and the U.S. airlift of arms to Israel, the Arab oil embargo, the rupture by Ethiopia under intense pressure of long-standing diplomatic relations with Israel,[75] and the entry of Somalia into the Arab League—all made it clear that U.S. policy options in the Horn had been radically reduced. It was in these circumstances of threats and tension, as the year 1974 opened, that the forty-four-year reign of Haile Sellassie finally collapsed.

The overthrow of Haile Sellassie can be attributed to various factors which can be explored only briefly in this study.[76] It was clear well in advance of the event that intolerable pressures were building up due to: (1) the failure of the Emperor to relax his hold on the parliament and the press in response to the aspirations for political modernization voiced by the university-educated younger generation and the rapidly growing trade union movement; (2) the impatience of the urban entrepreneurial groups with outmoded governmental controls; (3) the procrastination and insensitivity of aged cabinet and lower-rank officials in response to demands for reform; (4) corruption; (5) famine; and (6) the chaotic state of governmental and national finances brought on in part by the sudden soaring of Persian Gulf oil prices.

Yet, even more significant, in terms of U.S. relations, were two other factors. First, in a very real sense the civil government no longer existed, its ministers and top functionaries having been paralyzed and then drained of power by an aged spider clinging motionless to the center of a vast web of authority. Only the military escaped the net. The paralysis of civil authority was obvious to all foreign observers.

Second, the center of all power, the Emperor, refused to designate a successor, and his immobilism finally turned him into a twentieth-century Louis XV—*après moi le déluge*. Given his advanced age, not only the U.S.

---

[75] For a succinct account of this period, see Colin Legum, *Ethiopia: The Fall of Haile Selassie's Empire* (New York: Africana Publishing Co., 1975), p. 21.

[76] For fuller accounts, see the author's "Haile Selassie: Triumph and Tragedy," *Orbis*, Winter 1975, pp. 1129-1152; Legum, *op cit*.

government but even the ambitious Ethiopians who wanted to, and eventually would, overthrow him, felt it prudent to let events take their course. Both parties wanted to avoid giving rivals an excuse for intervening on behalf of the Emperor. Once the latter was gone, the contest for power could be fought out on even terms. And so it was that, from the first outbreak of violence in January 1974 until the death of the Emperor in August 1975, the United States followed a hands-off policy. During the critical period of political gestation of the regime about to take over, the United States rejected the Emperor's urgent requests for additional military assistance to meet external crises in Eritrea and the Ogaden and chose to be represented in Addis Ababa only by a chargé d'affaires. The fear of being identified with a repudiated ruler so persistently haunted U.S. policy that, in the end, Washington watched transfixed while the new regime took the path of communism rather than traditional alignment with the West.

These internal origins of revolutionary transformation are by no means unique to Ethiopia or to our times. It would be naive, however, to assume that they suffice to account for the vast changes. There are at least three reasons for believing that it was the encirclement of Ethiopia by the Arabs and Soviets in Eritrea and Somalia and her inability to respond to this challenge that were decisive in bringing about the upheaval.

In the first place, if the demands of interest groups, including the labor unions, the bureaucracy and the students, for liberal and democratic reforms were the cause of the revolution, they went unheeded in the new dispensation—unlike the tentative reforms following the abortive coup of 1960. The Derg which took over proceeded immediately in precisely the opposite direction, operating as a mysterious and tyrannical elite totally oblivious of what had been sought by the reformists. Its first act was to dissolve the parliament, and it then embarked upon a program of mass arrests and executions. It imprisoned the labor leaders, and soon the Confederation of Ethiopian Labor Unions (CELU) declared its open opposition to a regime that was suppressing civil rights.[77] By way of retaliation, the Derg next proclaimed a state of emergency.

Opposition mounted when the Derg issued the "Declaration on Economic Policy of Socialist Ethiopia," calling for nationalization and collectivization of farm lands, and announced the campaign for one year of service, zemetcha, under which all students would be sent into the countryside to educate the people in the new socialist philosophy. Even those peasants who expected to gain by the nationalization of all lands, found in

[77] Africa Confidential, October 10, 1975, pp. 1-3; October 8, 1976, p. 2; Le Monde (Sélection hebdomadaire), December 26, 1974-January 1, 1975; Marina Ottawa, "Social Classes and Corporate Interests in the Ethiopian Revolution," Journal of Modern African Studies, Vol. 14, No. 3 (1976), p. 484; Spencer, p. 1144.

the end that in place of former landlords they now had the government as landlord. The result has been desperate food shortages, particularly in Addis Ababa, due to the refusal of irate peasants to harvest crops for the new military landlord. After execution of some twenty farmers for refusing to bring food to the market, prices were reported to have fallen somewhat. Some 2,000 students were imprisoned for refusal to join in the *zemetcha* campaign ordered by the Derg. As a result of these measures, both the conservative EDU (Ethiopian Democratic Union) and the Marxist EPRP (Ethiopian People's Revolutionary Party) called for the overthrow of the Derg in order to institute a democratic regime.[78]

In the face of revolts throughout the country, repressions by the Derg took first the form of massive arrests and executions, followed by a series of purges within the army and, more recently, within the Derg itself—the most notable being the executions in July 1976 of Major Sisay Habte, Chairman of the Derg's Political and Foreign Affairs Committee, and of General Teferi Bante, Head of State, on February 3, 1977, who was suspected of seeking compromises with the Eritreans and the EPRP.[79]

In the second place, whatever the complaints against the monarchy, there had been general agreement among the various rival groups that attempts to resolve internal problems should await the installation of a new regime following the demise of the Emperor. The foreign challenges, on the other hand, had to be dealt with right away. The struggle with the ELF and the campaign of subversion pursued by the Arab states in Eritrea demanded the full attention of the military authorities in Addis Ababa. Indeed, it was the mutiny of the junior officers of the Second Division in Eritrea on February 26, 1974, that finally touched off the revolution.[80]

Since the February mutiny, the violence in Eritrea, nourished by Arab and Soviet money and arms, has constantly escalated, reaching a climax in May 1977 when the Sudan became an active participant. Military oper-

---

[78] *New York Times*, October 1, 3, 12, 21, 1975; *Washington Post*, October 1, 1975; Ottaway, p. 482; *Declaration on Economic Policy of Socialist Ethiopia* (Addis Ababa, February 7, 1975), pp. 1-11; *Ethiopian Herald*, March 23, 1975; *Africa Confidential*, May 23, 1975, p. 5; *Marchés Tropicaux*, April 18, 1975; *Manchester Guardian*, June 21, 1975; *Christian Science Monitor*, February 20, 24, 1975; *Le Monde*, February 11, 1977.

[79] *Christian Science Monitor*, February 24, 1976; *Observer*, February 29, 1976; *New York Times*, February 29, May 30, October 8, 16, 1976; *Africa Confidential*, December 19, 1974, pp. 2-6; May 13, 1977, p. 3; *Le Monde*, November 12, 1976; *Ethiopian Herald*, July 14, 1976.

[80] The Emperor's Representative in Eritrea was placed under house arrest and the Emperor's grandson, the deputy commander of the navy, had to flee from the naval center at Massawa. Shortly before the events in Eritrea, a revolt of junior officers had taken place in the south at Neghelli, followed by a demonstration by teachers and taxi drivers (the latter protesting the rise in petrol prices) and clashes with students in Addis Ababa. See Blair Thomson, *Ethiopia: The Country That Cut Off Its Head* (London: Robson Books, 1975), p. 22ff. See also *Africa Confidential*, March 8, 1974, p. 1; Colin Legum, *Africa Contemporary Record: Annual Survey and Documents, 1974-1975* (New York: Africana Publishing Co., 1975), p. B-160ff, and Legum, *The Fall of Haile Selassie's Empire*.

ations have included the bombing of villages, street fighting and terrorist mopping-up operations in Asmara, killing of prisoners, and destruction of crops and cutting off of food supplies to the civilian population. There has even been an accusation that the Derg had engaged in genocide against the Eritreans.[81] Perhaps nothing so dramatically illustrated the Derg's frustration as its abortive campaign for a "Farmers' March" or "Green Campaign," modeled on Morocco's moves to occupy former Spanish Sahara. This operation met with disaster. The unarmed peasants from northern Ethiopian provinces were, for the most part, taken prisoner in Eritrea but later released, although some of these, upon returning, were liquidated by the Derg. General Getachew Nadew, the Derg's martial law administrator for Eritrea, was executed by the Derg in July 1976. Thereafter, the ELF and the PLF, supplied with Soviet and Czech arms and captured U.S. weapons, gradually gained control of most of the Eritrean countryside, confining Ethiopian troops to the few remaining cities, such as Asmara and Keren. At the same time, the EDU was able to establish headquarters in the Gondar region of northwest Ethiopia. Faced with these challenges, the Derg announced in April 1977 a new mass mobilization of peasants to march against the EDU and Eritrean forces.[82]

A third source of foreign pressures were the Soviet and Somali threats to the Ogaden and the Djibouti territory. The executions of Major Sisay Habte and General Teferi Bante pointed to the Derg's long-standing fear lest the Soviets and Somalis profit from Ethiopia's failure to subdue the revolt in Eritrea by seizing the Ogaden and occupying the Djibouti territory. Understandably, the Derg had, from the outset, preferred Maoist socialism to Soviet communism, for Moscow had been supplying arms to the Eritrean dissidents and building in Somalia a power structure from which the Ogaden could be seized. Yet by early 1976, Soviet influence had advanced to the point that two pro-Soviet political movements had emerged in Ethiopia. One is the All-Ethiopia Socialist Movement, eventually adopted by the Derg as its politburo (renamed the Permanent Committee after the January 1977 reorganization), under the leadership of Haile Fida, a Marxist, educated in Paris.[83] The equally pro-Soviet EPRP (Ethiopian Peoples' Revolutionary Party), outlawed by the Derg, has pilloried the Derg as a 'fascist junta" "out to stifle democracy," "feudal-

---

[81] *Washington Post*, December 24, 25, 1974, February 3, 23, and July 30, 1975; *Africa Confidential*, September 12, 1975, p. 3; October 24, 1975, p. 8.

[82] *New York Times*, April 29 and May 1, 1977; *Washington Post*, April 22, 1977; *Africa Confidential*, May 13, 1977, p. 2.

[83] Among his associates in the Politburo have been Senaye Likke, Vice Chairman, educated at the University of Califorina; Melasse Ayalew, Brandeis; Wond Wossen Haile, Brandeis and Columbia; Assefa Medhede, University of California; and Ishetu Uchele, Syracuse University (private sources of information.) See *Africa Confidential*, May 28, 1976, p. 7.

ists," and an "imperialist puppet." It has accused Haile Fida of "CIA activities," and specifically charged that "Major Sisay Habte, the ultra right chief of the political commission of the Derg . . . has made no less than three trips to a number of West European countries. . . ."[84]

It was, therefore, remarkable that, in announcing the execution of Major Sisay Habte, the Derg should suddenly have adopted the EPRP accusations against him, declaring that he had "used this office as a cover to make contacts with agents of imperialists by going to countries where he had not been sent after changing his flight schedules whenever he was sent abroad on political missions," and that "he refused to undertake his revolutionary duty of leading a high-level delegation on an urgent national mission to the Soviet Union—exemplary founder of the socialist ideology. . . ."[85]

In announcing his execution, the Derg denounced U.S. and CIA influence in Ethiopia. This act, the sudden expulsion of all U.S. personnel except the Embassy staff,[86] and the acceptance by the Derg of the Soviet proposal by which Ethiopia would disappear in a federation extending from Eritrea to the People's Democratic Republic of Yemen, point to the decisive role that foreign threats and pressures have played in the revolution. The abrupt approach to the Soviets indicates that the Derg hoped in this way to dissuade the Soviets and the Somalis from taking advantage of the continued violence in Eritrea to invade the Ogaden and seize Djibouti.

The basis for effective cooperation between the United States and Ethiopia has disappeared. In the first place, collaboration with the regime of Haile Sellassie I had long been critically viewed, especially by the U.S. Congress, on the ground that the regime was autocratic and had failed to move with the times. There were no political parties, censorship was heavy, the elite were pampered, and the needs of the populace were ignored. Corruption within and outside the government was thought to be rampant. The national budget appeared to be heavily burdened by defense and the sybaritic expenditures of an insensitive Court.[87] Yet, so tyrannical is the present military dictatorship that the rule of Haile Sellassie I now seems positively liberal by comparison. Because of violations of human rights, U.S. aid was cut off completely in February 1977. Parliament has been dissolved. There is no constitution. Political parties and labor unions are proscribed. The one university in the country has

---

[84] *Abyot*, EPRP Publication No. 3, February-March 1976, pp. 1,5,10,13,14,15,18,20,22,25.

[85] *Ethiopian Herald*, July 14, 1976, p. 3.

[86] At this time, the EPRP campaign for a democratic civilian regime was gaining considerable support. *Africa Confidential*, October 8, 1976, p. 3.

[87] Much was made in Congress some years ago of the expense entailed for the American taxpayer in refurbishing, for the exclusive use of the Emperor, the captain's quarters on the flagship of the Ethiopian navy (a former U.S. seaplane tender).

been closed. Censorship of the press is no longer necessary, since the press itself has become an organ of the government.

Second, the internal violence and terror, and the setbacks in the Ogaden and Eritrea, strongly indicate that the viability of the Derg is in doubt. As in the last months of the Emperor's reign, cooperation with a possibly moribund regime would appear not to be profitable. Third, an even more horrendous picture has emerged in Eritrea with the kidnaping of Americans, bombings, executions and the burning of crops designed to produce mass starvation. To this, a new dimension has been added—the threat of a holy war waged by the Derg against the Eritrean Moslems—a forerunner of which may have been the "Farmers' March."[88]

A fourth obstacle is the Derg's strongly anti-American attitude. The announcement of Major Sisay's execution was accompanied by a dissertation drawing a parallel between Chile under Salvador Allende and present-day Ethiopia: "Chile's experience is a warning and a lesson for the oppressed masses of Ethiopia now engaged in advancing the cause of the on-going revolution."[89] At recent rallies, signs bearing the following slogans have appeared: "Ethiopia will never be another Chile," "Away with CIA agents disguised as tourists," "EPRP is a CIA organization." The anti-American campaign culminated on April 13, 1977, with the expulsion of all U.S. official personnel except the Embassy staff.

A fifth difficulty, associated with the anti-Americanism, is the Derg's sudden turn to the Soviet Union. Finally, Ethiopia's conflict with the radical Arab states over Eritrea and Greater Somaliland is scarcely compatible with the U.S. policy of accommodation of Arab states generally.

These factors have made it impossible for the United States to continue its arms deliveries to Ethiopia under the Mutual Defense Agreement of 1953—especially with respect to requests for additional deliveries of arms to replenish munitions expended in suppressing the revolt in Eritrea.[90] In addition, U.S. government officials indicated that supplying military assistance for this purpose might offend the oil-rich Arab states which are providing arms to the ELP/PLF.

---

[88] *Washington Post*, March 2, 14, April 1, May 4, 1977. Four Americans at Kagnew Station were kidnaped as a protest against the U.S. base in Eritrea; see *Department of State Bulletin*, April 7, 1975, p. 440.

[89] *Ethiopian Herald*, July 14, 1976, p. 2.

[90] For a report on the cash sale of $7 million worth of ammunition, see *Department of State Bulletin*, April 17, 1975; see also, *New York Times*, February 18, 1975; *Africa Confidential*, August 29, 1975, p. 4, and December 5, 1975, p. 8.

For the Primakov theory of U.S. relations with the Arab world, see testimony of Uri Ra'anan in U.S. Congress, Senate, Committee on Foreign Relations, *Proposed Sale of C-130s to Egypt*, Hearings before the Subcommittee on Foreign Assistance, 94th Cong., 2nd sess., April 1, 1976 (Washington, D.C.: GPO, 1976), pp. 61-62. According to this Soviet theory, the Atlantic Coast oil interests in the United States, which have a vast stake in Middle East oil, will ultimately prevail over the Gulf Coast oil interests in compelling the U.S. government to reach an accommodation with the oil-rich Arab states.

6.
The United States and Africa

THE DISASTROUS UNRAVELING of many decades of association with Ethiopia, during which the United States had enjoyed a position of unique preeminence, can be attributed largely to important considerations lying beyond the immediate realm of U.S.-Ethiopian relations. The United States has always, perhaps understandably, regarded Ethiopia as part of Africa and, therefore, as a proper object of U.S. African policy. Her struggle against the fascist invasion of 1935 was viewed as a harbinger of the eventual emergence of that continent to independence. Haile Sellassie's leadership of that struggle, his role as elder statesman, and the selection of Addis Ababa as headquarters of the OAU fortified that assessment. Yet, as Washington's attitude during the Italo-Ethiopian War demonstrated, U.S. policy toward Africa has been consistently one of non-involvement as contrasted with that toward other continents.

Four factors have produced this hands-off policy. In the first place, as distinguished from the "Open Door" policy reserved for the Far East, U.S. policy toward Africa has been that of the "Closed Door." In the Far East, the United States steadfastly refused to recognize any area as the colonial preserve of any European power or of Japan. On the contrary, in Africa, it acquiesced in the system of exclusionary regimes established by the Final Act of the Conference of Berlin in 1885. As compared to the Far East, Africa appeared to offer few commercial and still fewer strategic advantages. In consequence, so long as the United States continued to invoke the Monroe Doctrine to exclude European colonial powers from the Western Hemisphere, it felt compelled to accept the Closed Door on the continent of Africa. Liberia, for example, was founded by the American Colonization Society. Yet the United States withheld recognition until long after Britain and France had recognized it. On no fewer than seven occasions (1869, 1885, 1887, 1892, 1897, 1905 and 1907) it either ignored, or merely delivered polite protests against, seizures of Liberian territory by the British and the French.

In the 1950s a second factor appeared to support this closed-door, hands-off policy toward Africa, namely, NATO. It required that the United States avoid taking any position in respect to Africa which might embarrass or impair cooperation with NATO allies. For several years, the United States supported the colonial powers in their refusal to transmit to the UN General Assembly reports on political developments in their colonies, choosing to accept the latters' interpretation of Article 73e of the

UN Charter on this point. While professing fervent attachment to self-determination in Africa, U.S. votes at the UN supported the movement opposed to independence for Tunisia, Morocco, Algeria, Angola and Mozambique. Strategic deterrence required political deference. In 1957, Senator John F. Kennedy, in a speech calling for self-determination for Algeria, brought down on himself the criticism of both the Republican and Democratic leaders in Congress. Even after 1966, when all French territories in Africa but one had become independent and when France had repudiated her military commitments to NATO, the U.S. government continued to exhibit great restraint in supporting American commercial interests seeking to do business in those former colonies. That same NATO factor effectively precluded, until 1975, overt support for movements that might jeopardize Portuguese rule in Angola.

These first two factors led the United States to pursue a hands-off policy toward Africa. In other words, the policy was to "leave Africa to the Europeans, provided they leave the Western Hemisphere to us." The point was clearly put by Senator Mansfield in speaking of the crisis in the Congo in the 1960s:

It is necessary to bear in mind that the history of Africa is one of European involvement, not American. The mess in Africa is not of our doing, and while we cannot dissociate ourselves from major situations of this kind it would be most unfortunate if we were to be drawn into the internecine warfare of the Congolese. . . . The jungle of emergent African politics is marked with pitfalls for the unwary outsider. If we plunge into this difficulty on the mistaken assumption that we can resolve it or even influence its evolution without a massive involvement we may well pay an enormous price.[91]

This long-standing assessment that the United States should leave Africa to the Europeans has dictated a policy of strict non-involvement in the perennial problem of threats to the territorial integrity and unity of African states. The one exception has been the Cooperation Agreement of July 8, 1959, with Liberia, which provides for consultation in the case of aggression or threat of aggression against Liberia.[92] This provision contrasts strangely with the refusal of the United States to undertake the

---

[91] U.S. Congress, Senate, *Congressional Record*, August 21, 1964, 88th Cong., 2nd sess., Vol. 110, Pt. 16, p. 20884. Recently, Senator Humphrey observed: "We know so little about Africa, the 800 and some tribes that make up Africa. Where are the experts here in the Senate on the 800 and some cultural organizations or tribes in Africa? I have traveled in those countries, I say it is like a different world." *Ibid.*, December 17, 1975, 94th Cong., 1st sess., Vol. 121, No. 187, p. 22533.

For an attitude similar to Senator Mansfield's, see *Report to the President of the United States from the Committee to Strengthen the Security of the Free World* (The Clay Report), Department of State, March 20, 1963, pp. 9-10.

[92] Article I reads: "In the event of aggression or threat of aggression against Liberia, the Government of the United States of America and the Government of Liberia will immediately determine what action may be appropriate for the defense of Liberia."

defense of its own installation in Eritrea (Kagnew). The explanation may well be that the United States felt it could live with the Liberian agreement, since it did not expect that, on the eve of the departure of the French and the British from West Africa, NATO relationships would ever be involved; moreover, Washington probably felt that Liberia would not be attacked by continguous Guinea, following the conclusion the previous year of a boundary settlement between these countries, or by Sierra Leone or the Ivory Coast. What is unmistakable, however, is that an exceptional declaration of political support was given to Liberia.

This Liberian departure aside, the traditional policy of non-involvement in questions concerning the territorial integrity and independence of African states has marked the position of the United States in the Congo crises of 1961, 1965 and 1968; the Nigerian civil war of 1967-1968; the perennial Ethiopian-Somali-Eritrean conflicts; the Spanish Saharan issue, where the United States supported the partitioning of that country between Morocco and Mauritania;[93] and the invasion of the Shaba province of Zaire, where the U.S. contribution consisted of sending "nonlethal" spare parts for machine guns and transport equipment. On the contrary, France has played a leading role in African affairs. President Giscard d'Estaing declared at his press conference on April 12, 1977:

I wish to state that the Secretary of State of the United States passed through Paris last Saturday, that we talked in general terms of the situation in Africa, but that I did not inform him of our intention of eventually responding to the requests [for military assistance] which we might receive. In short, France is pursuing an independent policy. . . .
A change in the political situation in Africa, a general condition of insecurity or subversion in Africa would have consequences for France and Europe. That is why France wished—as I said a moment ago—to give a signal and, for my part . . . I prefer that that signal be given without any agreement with the United States. This is the time to show, for once, that there are some . . . situations where Europe should assert itself and Europe has asserted itself through France as its agent. . . . the importance of the African problem has been underscored by France on behalf of Europe."[94]

In substance, the United States has long held to the view that it has no basic strategic interests in Africa. Africa should be left to the Europeans, including the Russians.

A third factor was the belief that, even though it would be in the U.S. interest to keep communist activity out of that continent, the colonial

---

[93] See Thomas M. Franck, "The Stealing of the Sahara," *American Journal of International Law*, 1976, p. 718.
[94] *Le Monde*, April 14, 1977. See also, *ibid.*, April 23, 1977, and *Washington Post*, April 21, 1977, p. A-1.

regimes, while they lasted, would do just that. In fact, it was only in 1949 that the Soviet Union finally decided to undertake a serious study of African problems.[95] This inactivity afforded empirical support of Engel's doctrine that communism should refrain from efforts to detach the colonies from their metropoles. The theory was that, on the one hand, African colonies possessed neither the proletariat nor the bourgeoisie necessary to fuel the stages of the communist revolution. On the other hand, since the metropoles possess both of these classes, communist efforts should be concentrated there. The colonies would then fall with the metropoles into the embrace of communism, provided the colonial links had been maintained intact in the interval.[96] Advocates of the opposed theory argued, of course, that the metropoles were critically dependent upon their colonies and that activity designed to promote the latter's independence was possibly the most efficient means for hastening the end of capitalism in the metropoles.[97]

But it was Engel's theory that appeared to gain confirmation in practice. Communist activity in the colonies was minimal, and where it did appear, as in the Ivory Coast, it had been exported from the metropole.[98] In Tunisia, the communist WFTU succeeded for a time in crushing the nationalist movement. The Soviet Union under Khrushchev was notably slow, reluctant, and, in the end, apologetic about recognizing the independence of Algeria, hoping by this pro-metropole policy to entice France out of NATO and eventually to gain Algeria through France herself. In addition to the Engel theory, the Kremlin feared that promotion of independence movements might give dangerous ideas to the Soviet Union's own subject nationalities.[99] The Engel theory received brilliant confirmation in the case of Angola, which emerged into independence as a communist state following the radicalization of Portugal.

---

[95] Alexander Dallin, "The Soviet Union: Political Activity," in Zbigniew Brzezinski, editor, *Africa and the Communist World* (Stanford, Calif.: Stanford University Press, 1963), p. 10; Fritz Schatten, *Communism in Africa* (New York: Praeger, 1966), p. 102; Robert Legvold, *Soviet Policy in West Africa* (Cambridge, Mass.: Harvard University Press, 1970), pp. 1-39.

[96] Fritz Schatten, "Nationalism and Communism," in Walter Laqueur and Leopold Labedz, editors, *Polycentrism* (New York: Praeger, 1962), p. 237; cf. Dallin, p. 24.

[97] For Lenin's theory on this point, see Schatten, *Communism in Africa*, pp. 57-58, 78; Zbigniew Brzezinski, "How to Control a Deviation," *Encounter*, September 1963, pp. 77-89; H. Desfosses Cohn, *Soviet Policy Toward Black Africa* (New York: Praeger, 1972), p. 18.

[98] Ruth Schachter Morgenthau, *Political Parties in French-Speaking West Africa* (Oxford, England: Clarendon Press, 1964), p. 15; Aristede R. Zolberg, *One-Party Government in the Ivory Coast* (Princeton, N.J.: Princeton University Press, 1964), p. 75; Walter Kolarz, "The West African Scene," *Problems of Communism*, November-December 1961, p. 17.

[99] Willard A. Beling, "W.F.T.U. and Decolonization: A Tunisian Case Study," *Journal of Modern American Studies*, Vol. II, No. 4 (1964), pp. 556-560. "The French Communists themselves were hoping not only to retain, but to extend power in the center and thus, as it were, to capture the colonies via Paris." Kolarz, "The West African Scene," p. 17.

A fourth factor was the American calculation that, even after the colonial territories became independent, the strength of nationalism in such new states would be strong enough to prevent communist takeovers. This view, of which Senator Richard Clark (D., Iowa) is the chief protagonist, was first officially advanced in the (Clay) Report to the President of the United States from the Committee to Strengthen the Security of the Free World: "We believe that these new countries value their independence and do not wish to acquire a new master in place of the old one."[100] This "Clay" doctrine is by no means a demonstrable proposition.[101] On the contrary, evidence abounds to sustain the opposite view that nationalism does not constitute such a barrier. As Ho Chi Minh observed, "In Asia as elsewhere, Communism can develop no real political momentum unless it comes to terms with nationalism."[102] Rare are the exceptions in Africa where that accommodation has not taken place. Forms and models take precedence over ideologies in molding government structure in Black Africa. The single-party dictatorship, which has now become the sole acceptable form of government,[103] finds the Moscow model far more compatible than the Washington paradigm, with its bipartisan struggles and the long-standing NATO links with former colonial powers.

While the African states have been slow to adopt Marxist ideologies, they have found Soviet military presence and installations on their territories to be more compatible with, and less of a threat to, their independence than U.S. presence and installations. Whereas the United States has closed out its "facilities" in Morocco, Libya and Ethiopia, the Soviets have been using facilities in Libya, Guinea, Nigeria, Equatorial Guinea, the People's Republic of the Congo, Angola, Mozambique, Somalia, and the People's Democratic Republic of Yemen (Aden and Socotra), and supplying arms to these states and to Benin, Burundi, Central African Republic,

---

[100] *Report to the President . . . from the Committee to Strengthen the Security of the Free World*, p. 9.

[101] "So far from expecting a convergence of nationalism and communism in the underdeveloped countries, it is this author's belief that the ideological difference between them will become more important as the new societies approach the goal of industrial modernization." Richard Lowenthal, "Communism and Nationalism," *Problems of Communism*, November-December 1962, pp. 43-44.

[102] On the contrasting approaches of the Soviet Union (convergence) and the People's Republic of China (nonconvergence), see Brzezinski's *Encounter* article. See also Walter Laqueur, "Communism and Nationalism in Africa," *Foreign Affairs*, July 1961; George Padmore, *Pan-Africanism or Communism?* (London: Dobson, 1956); Franz Ansprenger, *Politik im Schwarzen Afrika* (Cologne: Deutscher-Verlag, 1961), pp. 436-444.

[103] "It is almost as though all of Africa south of the Sahara were permeated, as it were, by a mental blueprint of a despotic political structure, transmitted from generation to generation as a part of traditional verbal culture, and always available to be transmuted into reality whenever some individual arises with the imagination, enterprise, strength and luck to establish, with the aid of his kinsmen, an authoritarian regime over people residing beyond the limits of his local community." George Peter Murdock, *Africa: Its Peoples and Their Culture History* (New York: McGraw-Hill, 1959), p. 37.

Mali, Tanzania, Upper Volta and Zambia as well.[104] Despite the recent break between Moscow and Cairo, the Soviet Union still retains the use of Mersa Matruh and Alexandria, although on a limited basis. Faced with this preponderance of Soviet strength, the United States has withdrawn to Diego Garcia in the center of the Indian Ocean.[105] It would be difficult today to imagine any state in Africa that would accept two thousand American military "advisers" and "technicians" or a combined missile, naval and aircraft base of the importance of Berbera in Somalia. The Closed Door in Africa has proven to be a door closed to the United States but not to the Soviet Union with regard to strategic installations.

---

[104] See *New York Times*, December 10, 14, 1975, and January 19, 1976. Testifying before the Senate Committee on Armed Services, Admiral Noel Gayler, Commander-in-Chief, Pacific, remarked: "I heard someone likening them [the Soviets] to somebody running down a corridor trying every door and going in every one they found open." U.S. Congress, Senate, Committee on Armed Services, *Fiscal Year 1977 Authorization for Military Procurement, Research and Development, and Active Duty, Selected Reserve and Civilian Personnel Strengths*, Hearings, 94th Cong., 2nd sess., March 1, 1976 (Washington, D.C.: GPO, 1976), p. 4062.

[105] Withdrawal to Diego Garcia was accompanied by an announcement that the United States would sell approximately $300 million worth of arms to Ethiopia, Kenya and Zaire. Ethiopia would be permitted to purchase two squadrons of F-5Es, one squadron of F-5As, some M-60 heavy tanks, some C-130 cargo aircraft, as well as antitank weapons and armored personnel carriers, for a total of some $175 million. *Washington Post*, July 6, 1976.

7.
The United States, Ethiopia and the Middle East

RELATIONS BETWEEN the United States and Ethiopia have been essentially a function of this Closed Door policy. In the 1930s, that policy dictated a hands-off attitude toward the Italo-Ethiopian conflict during the preliminary stages when Britain and France were proposing the partitioning of Ethiopia as a means of keeping Italy in the Stresa Front. It also applied during the hostilities when the United States imposed an arms embargo on both belligerents and refrained from sanctions. Following the liberation of Ethiopia in 1941, the United States was rhetorically in favor of the territorial and political integrity of Ethiopia, reiterating that principle in the secret arms assistance agreement of 1960, but at all times rejecting any defense undertaking.[106] Thus, while it was opposed to the project for annexing the Ogaden to a Greater Somaliland, Washington preferred, in line with its African policy of strategic non-involvement, to walk away from the problem, as it did in the case of Eritrea, by phasing out arms assistance and its defense installation there. The Clay-Clark theory that the nationalism of a newly independent state would enable it to resist the blandishments of communism was apparently a factor in the U.S. decision to promote, in 1959, the first step along the road to a Greater Somaliland. Yet today, Somalia, ruled by the Marxist dictatorship of General Siad Barre, has become a client state of the Soviet Union. Similarly, in supporting the independence of that manifestly nonviable enclave, the Djibouti territory, the United States is still adhering to that theory of nationalism, although the chances for that territory to escape absorption by communist Somalia are slight.[107] While Ethiopia has declared that she will respect that independence, Somalia has refused to do so.

---

[106] See testimony of Assistant Secretary of State for African Affairs, David D. Newsom, in U.S. Congress, Senate, Committee on Foreign Relations, *U.S. Security Agreements and Commitments Abroad, Part 8, Ethiopia*, p. 1904.

[107] See testimony of Assistant Secretary of State for African Affairs, William E. Schaufele, Jr., in U.S. Congress, Senate, Committee on Foreign Relations, *Ethiopia and the Horn of Africa*, Hearings before the Subcommittee on Africa, 94th Cong., 2nd sess., August 6, 1976 (Washington, D.C.: GPO, 1976), pp. 116, 136. An indication that the United States might be entertaining second thoughts about the Clay doctrine may be noted in the fact that it has refrained from supporting independence for former Spanish Sahara. Independence is the goal sought for that territory by communist-oriented Algeria, whereas the United States has opted for partitioning between Morocco and Mauritania.

Whether or not the United States decides to take action to counter or compensate for Soviet hegemony in the Horn, a fresh approach toward Ethiopia is required. It no longer suffices to apply to Ethiopia policies adopted for the rest of Africa. The fact is that Ethiopia is an anomaly. Although situated in Africa and providing the headquarters of the Organization of African Unity, she must be regarded as more a part of the Middle East than of Africa.[108] All of her problems have arisen and can be solved only in the former context.

As the only independent state in black Africa—apart from Liberia—until the 1950s, she was completely cut off from that continent by the colonial regimes, except for the foreign commerce that passed through Djibouti and the seasonal trade with the Sudan at the enclave of Gambeila on the Baro River.[109] Following the era of independence in the 1960s, Ethiopia's relations with black Africa have been consistently on a friendly basis, as evidenced by the selection of Addis Ababa as headquarters of the OAU and the unusually active role played by Haile Sellassie I as elder statesman.[110] Her leadership in the struggle against colonialism has been gratefully remembered by Africa south—less so by Africa north—of the Sahara. In short, Ethiopia's problems lie elsewhere. Today, surrounded by members of the Arab League, except for the relatively short frontier with Kenya, Ethiopia has experienced problems only with the former, none with black Kenya.

In a sense, Ethiopia is probably more closely identified with the Arab world of the Middle East than are some Arab countries. "The Arab world is made up of four natural regions: the Fertile Crescent . . ., the Arabian peninsula, the Nile valley and the northern coast of Africa."[111] Ethiopia

---

[108] In his statement to the House subcommittee (*U.S. Policy and Request for Sale of Arms to Ethiopia*, p. 13), George W. Bader argued that "we have to look at Ethiopia not just as a part of Africa, but look at it as a central area and a greater region that would include the Arabian Peninsula and the Persian Gulf, Indian Ocean."
    Ambassador Mulcahy, on the same occasion (p. 13), informed the Congressmen that "The Ethiopians, themselves, have long been oriented towards the Middle East. . . . It has really until recent years tended to face more toward the Middle East than southward to black Africa." For a contrary view, see Hess, p. 215.

[109] For example, Ethiopian officials consistently refused, except under extreme necessity, to travel to Kenya because of the severe color bar restrictions. Ethiopian Airline operations were hampered for the same reason: Ethiopian pilots and personnel objected to going there during the colonial regime.
    Isolation of territories was also characteristic of colonial black Africa. Representatives of adjoining anglophone and francophone states often met for the first time when appointed delegates to the UN General Assembly.

[110] See Berhanykun Andemicael, *The OAU and the UN* (New York: Africana Publishing Co., 1976), pp. 51, 56, 59, 79, 81, 82, 88.

[111] J.C. Campbell, *Defense of the Middle East* (New York: Praeger, 1960, revised edition), p. 307. The UN Ad Hoc Committee on the Middle East produced this list of states considered to belong to the Middle East: Afghanistan, Iran, Iraq, Syria, Lebanon, Turkey, Saudi Arabia, Yemen, Egypt, Ethiopia and Greece. E/1360 and E/AC, 26/16. See also Roderick H. Davison, "Where is the Middle East?," in Richard H. Nolte, editor, *The Modern Middle East* (New York: Atherton Press, 1963), p. 25 n.

has traditionally belonged to two of these four parts: the Arabian penin-
sula—where the dominant Ethiopian race, culture and language (the
Amharic language, a Semitic tongue, is closely related to Arabic and
Hebrew) originated—and the Nile valley. For 1,500 years the seat of her
Coptic Christian Church was in Alexandria. Her Monophysite Christianity is shared by the Christian populations in Egypt, Syria and Lebanon.
For centuries the Ottoman Empire sought to overrun Ethiopia. Turkish
and Egyptian incursions ranged as far as southeast Ethiopia in the 1880s.
Despite a series of defeats administered to the Egyptian armies at Arkiko
(1844), Harar, Gura and Gundet in 1875-1876, Islamic attacks were
brought to a halt only after the intrusion of the colonial powers in the
1880s.[112]

At the Paris Peace Conference of 1946, Egypt still laid claim to Eritrea.
Nasser's campaign for the Unity of the Valley of the Nile, including the
three Somalilands (Italian, British and French) and Eritrea, reflected a
substantial hydrographic reality. Ethiopia is the ganglion of the network
of rivers that radiate outwards—northeast, southeast and south to the
three Somalilands, and west and northwest to the Sudan and Egypt. As
noted earlier, Ethiopia supplies 100 per cent of the waters of the three
Somalilands and over 80 per cent of those of the Nile in Egypt. Following
the return of Eritrea in 1952, Ethiopia's location on the western shores of
the Red Sea assumed critical importance to the Arab world. She had
thereby re-acquired a coastline of over 500 miles from the border of the
Sudan down to the Strait of Bab el Mandeb opposite the island of Perim[113]
and, with that coastline, the pelagic archipelago that lies astride the line of
shipping through the Red Sea to Suez and the Gulf of Aqaba. That unique
situation could not be ignored by her Arab neighbors who still want to
turn the Red Sea into an Arab lake.

The two sources of conflict in the Horn—(1) the Greater Somaliland
Movement for the incorporation of the Ogaden, Djibouti and the Red Sea
coast up to Massawa, and (2) the secession movement in Eritrea—must, in
the final analysis, be viewed in a Middle East (Arab) rather than an African
context. The non-Arab members of the Organization of African Unity
are fearful about the implications of both issues. It is the Arab states, both

---

[112] See M. Abir, *Ethiopia: The Era of Princes, 1769-1885* (London: Longmans, Green and Co., 1968);
Zewde Gabre-Sellassie, *Yehannes IV of Ethiopia* (Oxford, England: Clarendon Press, 1975), especially
Chapter II, "Egyptian Ambitions in Ethiopia." William Dye, an officer in the American Civil War who,
in the Reconstruction Period, sought his fortune in Egypt, the Sudan and Ethiopia, wrote: "So deep,
however, has been the impression made by them [Turks and Circassians] upon the Abyssinian, that he
looks on them as his natural enemies, and every foreigner who today enters the country is called a
Turk and believed to be a veritable one unless there is indisputable evidence to the contrary." *Moslem
Egypt and Christian Abyssinia* (New York: Atkin and Prout, 1880), pp. 39-40.

[113] The channel on the Ethiopian side of Perim (Ras Doumei'rah) is far wider and deeper (183 fathoms
maximum depth versus 21 fathoms) than the channel on the Yemen Arab Republic's side.

members and nonmembers of the OAU, that have supported the Greater Somaliland Movement and, to that end, admitted Somalia to membership in the Arab League. The secessionist movement in Eritrea was launched and supported by the Arab states, first by Egypt, then by the radical Arab states, and now by Egypt, the Sudan and Saudi Arabia. All have sought to expel non-Arab Ethiopia from the shores of the Red Sea.[114]

Certainly, there can be no opposition on the part of the OAU toward treating the problems of the Horn as Middle Eastern rather than African. In fact, the OAU has demonstrated a remarkable reluctance to embarrass itself with the problems of the Horn.[115]

At its inception in 1963 the OAU appeared to offer a forum for the problems of the Ogaden and Eritrea, for the OAU Charter, largely of Ethiopian inspiration, highlighted the principle of respect for territorial integrity and existing frontiers. Perhaps out of concern that these provisions of the OAU Charter might favor Ethiopia over Somalia, the latter, with the encouragement of the Soviet Union, sought to raise the problem of the Ogaden before the Security Council. Following pressure by the OAU in early 1964, however, Somalia decided to withdraw the matter from the United Nations and place it before the OAU. The result was disastrous for Somalia, since the OAU not only rejected the request, but went on to adopt Resolution 16(I), pledging the members "to respect the borders existing on their achievement of national independence."[116] A government crisis promptly ensued in Mogadiscio, and, since then, the OAU has carefully refrained from direct involvement in the dispute. Following an initial call to Somalia and Ethiopia to try to settle the matter directly, the problem has remained on the periphery of the OAU agenda, except for periodic exhortations to the parties. Finally, in 1973, over Ethiopian opposition, the OAU established a committee of reconciliation of seven members, which has so far failed to make any progress.

With respect to the secession movement in Eritrea, Ethiopia herself has opposed discussion of it in the OAU, alleging that it is a matter of domestic

---

[114] The Derg has recently delivered bitter attacks on the Arab states for their alleged efforts to create an Arab Eritrea on the shores of the Red Sea. The Ethiopian delegate to the Afro-Arab Summit Conference in Cairo in March 1977 declared: "There is a dream of making the Red Sea an Arab lake. The only part of the coasts of that sea that is not Arab is in Eritrea, and the Arab countries want to put an end to that situation." *Washington Post*, March 12, 1977, p. A8. At the same time, an Ethiopian government spokesman remarked: "It is an insult to the honor and dignity to [sic] the whole of Africa that some reactionary Arab countries along the Red Sea and far-off places should ignore the existence of a sovereign independent African state along the Red Sea coast." *New York Times*, March 16, 1977, p. 13.

[115] Andemicael (p. 58) remarks that the OAU has preferred to stand aside from disputes between member states on the theory that "African solidarity may be threatened more by an active involvement ... than by a modest role."

[116] RES AHG/16 (I), *OAU Resolutions and Recommendations of the First Session of the Assembly Heads of State and Government*, Provisional Secretariat of the OAU, Addis Ababa, p. 52. See also Zdenek Cervenka, *The Organization of African Unity* (London: C. Hurst, 1968); Andemicael, pp. 53-56.

jurisdiction outside the competence of the organization. The Arab members of both the OAU and UN oppose any raising of the Eritrean question by Ethiopia for a different reason: they fear it will lead to a discussion of their intervention with arms and funds in support of a secession movement. Nevertheless, at the OAU summit conference of 1973, Libya accused Ethiopia of being an ally of Zionism and an imperialist state faithless to African traditions for opposing the aspirations of the Somalis for a Greater Somaliland and the Eritreans for independence. He called for the removal of OAU headquarters from Addis Ababa. In 1975, as noted earlier, Ethiopia broke off relations with Tunisia when the latter sought to give the ELF official observer status at OAU meetings.

The United Nations could not be expected to examine these questions objectively. The Arab and Soviet groups would oppose discussion of their interventions and would effectively preclude any recourse by Ethiopia or by others. In the case of Eritrea, there is the additional factor that, following her unilateral suppression of the federation stipulated by UN Resolution 390(V), Ethiopia is scarcely in a position to seek a hearing at the United Nations.[117] In short, Arab influence in the OAU and the UN is dominant on all questions concerning Ethiopia.

Only rarely has the United States treated Ethiopia as part of the Middle East. During World War II, Ethiopia was recognized as falling under the jurisdiction of the Anglo-American Middle East Supply Center. Ethiopia was included in the Middle East for the purposes of the Eisenhower Doctrine;[118] and the Richards Mission, set up to implement the doctrine, was sent to Ethiopia along with other countries of the Middle East.

In contrast with its Closed Door policy for Africa, the United States has been actively involved in the Middle East since World War II. In the 1950s, while deferring to British hegemony in East Africa, the United States was pressing Britain to surrender its domination of Egypt and the Suez Canal—a policy that contributed to the confrontation of 1956 at Suez.[119] Subsequently, it was the United States that took the initiative in

---

[117] In an interview published by Le Monde, the leader of the ELP-PLF was asked: "Do you think the UN could help you in your struggle?" Answer: "Certainly not at this time. If we seize independence by force, the UN will recognize the fait accompli. But at the present stage of our struggle, that organization will do nothing for us." "And the Organization of African Unity?" Answer: "The OAU is even less disposed to help us than the UN. Only a military victory could bring that organization, like the UN, to recognize our existence." Le Monde, March 16, 1977.

[118] See Nolte, p. 14, and Campbell, p. 127.

[119] Writing of the events and attitudes of the United States already in 1953, Eden was particularly explicit on this point: "Anglo-American differences about Egyptian policy persisted. In a report home on the year, our Ambassador in Cairo commented that American policy in general seemed to be conditioned by a belief that Egypt was still the victim of British 'colonialism,' and as such deserving of American sympathy. It also appeared to be influenced by a desire to reach a quick solution almost at any cost and by a pathetic belief that, once agreement was reached, all would be well. These considerations,

establishing CENTO, which Britain joined at Washington's request. The U.S. commitment to Israel has required continued American involvement in Middle East and Red Sea diplomacy. Indeed, the Defense Installations Agreement of 1953 with Ethiopia served to enhance the flexibility of U.S. responses in the area.

This review of Ethiopia and the Horn of Africa as essentially a Middle East problem indicates that the United States has been wrong in treating the area as an African problem—and, thus, in applying a closed-door, hands-off policy to the strategic Horn of Africa. Nowhere in the Middle East has the United States assumed, as it had for Africa, that independence alone sufficed to constitute a barrier against communism. The Baghdad Pact was based on precisely the opposite assumption, and U.S. support for various Arab and non-Arab states is based on the premise that such friendly states must be strengthened to safeguard their independence and prevent communist expansion.

combined with a horror of unpopularity and fear of losing their influence with the new regime, particularly on the part of the United States Embassy in Cairo, and also an apparent disinclination by the United States Government to take second place even in an area where primary responsibility was not theirs, resulted in the Americans, at least locally, withholding the wholehearted support which their partner in N.A.T.O. had the right to expect and which would have been of great, if not decisive, influence on our negotiations. Inevitably the Egyptians exploited the equivocal American attitude." Anthony Eden, *Full Circle* (Boston, Mass.: Houghton Mifflin, 1960), pp. 284-285; see also, pp. 255 ff, 260, 264, 280.

8.
Soviet Objectives and Options

A^s THE SUCCESS of their policies suggests, the Soviets have not been handicapped by the misconceptions of the Horn of Africa that afflicted U.S. policy. Moscow rapidly perceived that the key to the mastery of the area lay with the Arabs and their implacable support of Eritrean independence and of the Greater Somaliland Movement, as well as their hostility toward Ethiopia for her relations with Israel. In 1977, however, now that it has acquired Ethiopia as a client state, the Soviet Union has come to oppose Eritrean independence—thus completely reversing its long-standing policy on this issue. To understand this significant twist in Soviet policy, we must examine the Kremlin's interests in and policies toward the area over the past several years.

It was the Soviet Union for the most part, and to a lesser extent the People's Republic of China, that supplied the arms for the Arab interventions in Eritrea. These have included AK-47 Kalaschnickov assault rifles, RPG-2 rocket launchers, 60mm mortars, and surface-to-air missiles, SAM-7s.[120] In the face of this buildup of Soviet arms in Eritrea and of a campaign directed against the U.S. defense installation there (Kagnew), congressional pressure began to develop in Washington in 1970 calling for U.S. withdrawal. In 1973, just after the Yom Kippur War, it was announced that the United States and Ethiopia had agreed to close out that defense installation.[121]

In addition to seeking American withdrawal from the area, the Soviet Union has an interest in establishing "denial-control" over shipping through the Red Sea. From the time of the Czars, Russia has sought the ice-free connection, which the Indian Ocean provides, between her Black Sea, Baltic and Arctic ports, and her ports in the Far East. The Suez Canal and the Red Sea offer Soviet vessels traveling from the Black Sea to the Indian Ocean a route that is about 70 per cent shorter in distance than the one around the Cape of Good Hope.[122] It is also through the Red Sea that

---

[120] *Africa Confidential*, November 27, 1970, pp. 5-6, and April 11, 1975, p. 6; *New York Times*, November 2, 1975, p. 26; *Africa*, April 1975, p. 11.

[121] Abir, "The Contentious Horn of Africa," p. 9; *Africa Report*, March-April 1975, p. 17; *Africa Confidential*, November 2, 1973, p. 1. The kidnapings of U.S. personnel at Asmara by the ELF in 1975 were designed to hasten the closing down of an installation whose presence had tended to discourage secessionist activities.

[122] Secretary of Defense James R. Schlesinger testified before the Senate Armed Services Committee on June 10, 1975, that the re-opening of the Suez Canal reduces the distance from the Black Sea to the Arabian Sea from 11,500 miles to only 2,500 miles—a difference in sailing time of 24 days. U.S. Congress, Senate, Committee on Armed Services, *Disapprove Construction Projects on the Island of Diego*

oil flows from the Persian Gulf to Israel at the end of the Gulf of Aqaba and to the Suez Canal and thence to Western Europe. In order to establish denial-control over Red Sea shipping, it is important for Moscow to gain control over the Eritrean coastline, over its offshore archipelago and its pelagic islands astride the main shipping lane through the Red Sea, and over the Eritrean side of the Strait of Bab el Mandeb. For this reason, the Kremlin is now supporting its client Ethiopian government, the Derg, in its struggle against the ELF, the Sudan and Saudi Arabia to retain that coastline and its islands. During Lt. Colonel Mangistu's visit to Moscow in May 1977, then President Podgorny openly revealed the Soviet Union's ambition in the usual communist manner of asserting that it is the "imperialists" who are doing it:

Insofar as the Red Sea is concerned, recent events prove that the imperialists seek to establish their control over this region with the assistance of certain Arab countries, primarily Saudi Arabia, in violation of the legitimate rights of other states and peoples in this region and to the detriment of free international navigation.[123]

On the other hand, the Soviets have had an even greater interest in consolidating a position of strength in Somalia. The long Somali coastline, jutting eastward into the Indian Ocean south of the entrance to and exit from the Red Sea, holds for them three attractions: (1) It dominates the oil life-lines from the Persian Gulf not only to the Gulf of Aqaba and the Suez Canal, but also to Europe and the United States around the Cape of Good Hope. (2) It protects Soviet access to the Indian Ocean through the Suez Canal and the Red Sea. (3) It controls the critical northwest quadrant of the Indian Ocean to which, for over a century, Imperial Russia and the Soviet Union have sought access, and over which the Kremlin is seeking control today. The increasing range of U.S. SLBMs (submarine-launched ballistic missiles), which could enable an American attack submarine operating in the Gulf of Aden to reach targets as far away as Murmansk and Lake Baikal, makes "sea denial" of the waters off the Horn of Africa an imperative for the Soviet Union.[124] Somalia itself offers a fourth and even more attractive possibility, that of transforming Ethiopia into a client state.

Garcia, Hearings on Senate Resolution 160 to Disapprove Construction Projects on the Island of Diego Garcia, 94th Cong., 1st sess. (Washington, D.C.: GPO, 1975), p. 8.

See also, Geoffrey Jukes, *The Indian Ocean in Soviet Naval Policy* (London: International Institute for Strategic Studies, Adelphi Paper No. 87, May 1972); Alvin J. Cottrell and R.M. Burrell, "Soviet-U.S. Naval Competition in the Indian Ocean," *Orbis*, Winter 1975; and K. P. Misra, "International Politics in the Indian Ocean," *ibid.*

[123] *Le Monde*, May 6, 1977. For similar language in the joint communique of May 9, 1977, issued in Moscow, see *ibid.*, May 10, 1977.

[124] Jukes, p. 6; Stansfield Turner, "The Naval Balance: Not Just a Numbers Game," *Foreign Affairs*, January 1977, p. 342.

With a military base established in Somalia and Somalian troops supplied with arms, tanks and transport, the Soviets are in position to exploit the secessionist movement in Eritrea by allowing Somalia to invade the Ogaden. This threat has been made even more plausible by the explosion of internal violence and opposition to the Derg in Ethiopia and the withdrawal of military assistance by the United States. If the Derg hopes to stave off the present invasion of the Ogaden, the loss of Eritrea and its own demise, it must turn, as it has now done, to the Soviets.

If Ethiopia is transformed fully into a client state, three important advantages would accrue to the Soviets. (1) They would be able to acquire a direct overland connection through the Ogaden between their bases at Mogadiscio and Berbera, which would be some 1,000 miles shorter than the sea route around the Horn; and the distance between Djibouti and Mogadiscio would be reduced by some 1,200 miles.

(2) They would be able to achieve their important objectives along the Red Sea coast, and in this connection the Derg would be given direct military assistance in order to put down the secessionist movement in Eritrea. That is precisely what is happening today, despite the fact that the Soviets have hitherto been supplying arms and funds to the ELF-EPLF and the independence movement has long been pro-Marxist. The evidence of this transformation has been the sudden turning of all three factions of the Eritrean liberation forces against the Soviet Union and toward the United States and the conservative Arab states of the Sudan and Saudi Arabia for support.[125]

(3) They would be establishing a degree of control over all of northeast Africa, because Ethiopia provides 100 per cent of the water resources of Somalia and Djibouti and 80 per cent of those of the Sudan and Egypt. Under these circumstances, it is understandable that both of these two countries have viewed with deep concern the recent turn of events in Ethiopia. With Libya, adjoining both the Sudan and Egypt, now cooperat-

---

[125] *New York Times*, November 2, 1975, p. 26, June 26, 1977, p. 12; *Washington Post*, June 9, 1977, p. A-16. See interview with Sabbeh Saleh, leader of the ELF and PLF, in *Le Monde*, March 16, 1977: "After sixteen years of war, which are, according to you, the countries which have furnished Eritrea the greatest assistance in its struggle for liberation?" "Iraq and Syria have helped us from the start and have never ceased to aid us. For a long time, Libya gave us important military assistance, but recently, despite my personal contacts with President Kadhafi, Libya has not only cut off that assistance, but has actually gone to the support of Ethiopia. Kuwait, Qatar, Abu Dhabi are helping us and we place great hopes in the assistance of the Riad government which Prince Saoud, the Foreign Minister, has himself formally promised."
"You have recently pointed to the presence of Cubans who, according to you, are apparently fighting in Eritrea alongside the Ethiopian troops. Does this mean that you do not exclude the possibility of a Soviet-Cuban intervention in the eastern Horn of Africa, like that which took place in Angola?" "The route for oil passes through the Red Sea; neither the producing countries nor the United States could ever abandon the eastern horn of the African continent to the Soviets or their Cuban friends. If Havana or Moscow should intervene militarily in Eritrea, the Arab world would not remain indifferent."

ing closely with the Soviet Union, Moscow would be in a good position to offset U.S. influence in the Middle East.[126]

In view of these calculations, it is scarcely surprising that the Soviet Union's first step in the Horn of Africa was an all-out effort to convert Somalia into a client state.[127] As distinguished from Eritrea, where the Soviets relied on Ethiopia's radical Arab neighbors to advance their interests, the USSR introduced arms directly into Somalia and without pretense built up its power base there. Once the Italian Trusteeship Administration had withdrawn in 1960, the Soviets swiftly took advantage of the tension between Somalia and Ethiopia over the Greater Somaliland issue by concluding a series of military aid agreements in 1963, 1966 and 1974, and economic and cultural agreements in 1961.[128] On the basis of these agreements, the Soviet Union had, by 1975, built up a military force in Somalia more powerful and modernized than that created in Ethiopia by the United States over a much longer period under the 1953 defense agreement.[129]

By 1974, the Soviet Union had established a naval, communications and missile base at Berbera on the north Somali coast opposite Aden and to the east of Djibouti, defended by SAM batteries. Facilities also now exist at Mogadiscio in Somalia; at Socotra, the island off the tip of the Horn of Africa; at Aden and the airport nearby; at Hodeida on the North Yemen coast; at Umm Qasir in Iraq, and at Mauritius.[130] In this manner, the entire northwest quarter of the Indian Ocean from the Gulf of Aden to Sri Lanka is surrounded by Soviet bases and facilities. The base at Berbera was built contrary to UN Resolution 2832 XXVI,[131] proclaiming the

[126] See the *New York Times*, August 10, 1976; *Washington Post*, January 28, 1977, A-1; *Le Monde*, May 6, 1977.

[127] During the 1975 drought the Soviet air force lifted over 100,000 peasants and their belongings from the stricken interior to settle them along the coast. *New York Times*, July 12, 13, 1975.

[128] *ARB* 1966, p. 623B; *Africa Confidential*, April 13, 1973, pp. 3-4; Touval, *Boundary Politics*, pp. 146-147; *Washington Post*, October 31, 1974.

[129] See *The Military Balance 1975-1976* (London: International Institute for Strategic Studies, 1976), p. 43; *Washington Post*, April 16, 1977, p. A-16; *Africa Confidential*, April 13, 1973, p. 4, and July 6, 1973, pp. 2-3; René Bénezra, "La Corne de l'Afrique: Un cap dangereux," *Afrique Contemporaine*, July-August 1975, pp. 5-6; J. Bowyer Bell, Jr., *The Horn of Africa: Strategic Magnet in the Seventies* (New York: Crane, Russak, 1973), pp. 41-43.

[130] UN Doc. A/AC 159/1, May 3, 1974, *Report on Declaration of the Indian Ocean as a Zone of Peace*, Resolution 2832XXVI and A/AC 159/1 Rev. 1, July 11, 1974 (same title). See testimony of Admiral Elmo Zumwalt, Jr., in U.S. Congress, House, Committee on Foreign Affairs, *Proposed Expansion of U.S. Military Facilities in the Indian Ocean*, Hearings before the Subcommittee on the Near East and South Asia, 93rd Cong., 2nd sess., February 21-March 20, 1974 (Washington, D.C.: GPO, 1974), pp. 129-158; and U.S. Congress, Senate, Committee on Foreign Relations, *Briefings on Diego Garcia and Patrol Frigate*, 93rd Cong., 2nd sess., April 11, 1974 (Washington, D.C.: GPO, 1974), pp. 2-19. See, also, testimony of Rear Admiral Charles D. Grojean, U.S. Congress, House, Committee on Appropriations, *Second Supplemental Appropriations Bill*, 1974, 93rd Cong., 2nd sess., March 8, 1974 (Washington, D.C.: GPO, 1974), pp. 64-85; and U.S. Congress, Senate, Committee on Appropriations, *Report to the Committee on Appropriations, U.S. Senate, by Members of the Fact-Finding Team, Sent to Somalia at the Invitation of the President of Somalia*, Committee Print, 94th Cong., 1st. sess., July 14, 1975.

[131] GAOR, Twenty-Sixth Session, Supplement No. 29 (A/8429), pp. 36-37.

Indian Ocean as a zone of peace and calling upon the great powers and the littoral states to eliminate all bases, military installations and logistical supply stations from the region. It was not surprising, therefore, that President Ford's revelation of Soviet construction of bases and facilities at Berbera and surrounding territories should have met with indignant denials by both the Soviets and the Somalis. However, the massive documentation established by the UN Report on the implementation of General Assembly Resolution 2832 XXVI, the hearings held by various committees of the House of Representatives, and the visit of members of Congress to the area fully confirm the existence of the Berbera and other installations.[132] It should be noted that the Soviet Union has now denied to the Somalis access to parts of the base at Berbera.

Within slightly over a decade, the Soviet Union has converted Somalia into a client state and a power base at the corner of the Indian Ocean and the Red Sea. The closing on March 31, 1977, of Britain's staging post at Massirah Island (Oman) means that the Soviets have replaced the former British presence in the Persian Gulf, Indian Ocean and Red Sea region with their own. Withdrawal from Massirah is suggestive. In its position relative to the Indian Ocean, the Strait of Hormuz and the Persian Gulf, Oman is strikingly analogous to the position of Somalia relative to the Indian Ocean, the Strait of Bab el Mandeb and the Red Sea. Should the Soviet Union eventually acquire facilities on Massirah, it would be gaining a position geographically analogous to Mogadiscio. Obtaining Ras Masadam on the western shores of the Strait of Hormuz would be analogous to gaining control of the Ethiopian side (Ras Doumeïrah) of the Strait of Bab el Mandeb. Further analogy is to be found in the Iranian possession of the islands of Musa and Greater and Lesser Tunb,[133] which lie just inside the Persian Gulf from the Strait of Hormuz, and the Ethiopian archipelago, which lies in the Red Sea about 100 miles north of the Strait of Bab el Mandeb.

Soviet facilities and bases around the continent of Africa and the shores of the Indian Ocean have, with but one exception, been confined to coastal installations.[134] That exception is Somalia, where the fumaroles of Mogadiscio and Berbera reveal the existence of massive military support facilities. The extent of this development in the context of Soviet world-

---

[132] *New York Times*, April 9, 1973; *Africa Report*, January-February 1975, p. 8; *Africa Confidential*, September 12, 1975, p. 5.

[133] Occupied by Iran on November 30, 1971. See *Washington Post*, January 24, p. A-10, February 18, p. A-24, May 14, p. A-12, 1977.

[134] "In 1973, Admiral Sergeev, Chief of the Soviet Naval Staff, was asked by a Western naval attaché what his greatest problem was as the result of the shift to forward deployment. He replied without hesitation: 'Bases.'" U.S. Congress, Senate, Committee on Commerce and National Ocean Policy, *Soviet Oceans Development*, Study pursuant to S. Res. 222, Committee Print, 94th Cong., 2nd sess., October 1976, p. 146.

wide programs was revealed during the hearings held by the Senate Committee on Armed Services on military construction authorizations for fiscal year 1975. Senator John C. Culver (D., Iowa) had addressed the following question to the Department of Defense: "List all locations outside the Warsaw Pact where the USSR has missile support facilities in being or under construction comparable to Berbera (or something similar)." The reply of the Pentagon was: "There are no known locations, other than Berbera, where the Soviets have similar missile support facilities."[135]

If the objective of the Soviet Union is to establish its presence in Africa and the Indian Ocean area, why should the bases at Mogadiscio and Berbera not be similar to those symbols of Soviet presence elsewhere on the periphery of Africa and the Indian Ocean, i.e., without inland military support facilities? Why should Berbera, for example, not resemble Aden, a naval and air facility without inland support? Why not build a missile base at Aden instead of one at Berbera—or even in addition to one at Berbera? Insofar as control of sea routes is concerned, why is Aden not as valuable for this purpose as Berbera? These questions are pertinent, for it is Berbera and Mogadiscio, rather than Aden, that "benefit" from the massive military build-up. If it is the capability to engage in "denial control" of traffic moving into and out of the Red Sea[136] that is important rather than a military "presence," why were the military support supplies and facilities furnished to Mogadiscio and Berbera in Marxist Somalia, rather than to Aden in the Marxist People's Democratic Republic of Yemen?

The answer may be, in part, a Soviet concern that a military concentration in the lower Arabian peninsula would constitute too great an abuse of the sensibilities of neighboring Saudi Arabia, Oman, Kuwait and Iran, whereas an Ethiopia, riven by internal conflict and unable to obtain matching military support, is in no position to object. In other words, expansion in the Horn of Africa is less costly in political-diplomatic terms for the Soviet Union than it would be on the Arabian coast.

However, the basic reason for the unusual inland expansion of Soviet military capabilities lies elsewhere—in the objective of gaining control of Ethiopia and, through it, control over the water resources of the Horn, the Sudan and Egypt, and over the Eritrean coasts and islands.

---

[135] U.S. Congress, Senate, Committee on Armed Services, *Military Construction Authorization for Fiscal Year 1975*, Hearings, 94th Cong., 1st sess., June 10, 1975 (Washington, D.C.: GPO, 1975), p. 68. On the prospective development of a capacity to project power ashore, see Turner, p. 342.

[136] Turner, p. 344ff. "It is significant that the Soviets have chosen to station a *Nanuchka*-class missile patrol boat at Berbera, a unit which is well suited to the task of preventing passage through these approaches [southern approaches to the Red Sea]." U.S. Congress, Senate, *Soviet Oceans Development*, p. 148. In addition, such "control" presumably could be exercised by naval units supplied to the radical Arab states, in particular, Somalia.

The Department of Defense is seriously concerned about Soviet "control" objectives and the highly strategic nature of the bases in Somalia. At the hearings of the Senate Committee on Armed Services on June 10, 1975, General George S. Brown, Chairman of the Joint Chiefs of Staff, testified:

The strategic importance of the Indian Ocean is derived, not only from its relationship to oil and mineral resources, but also from the air and sea lanes of communications running through it. . . . The energy needs of the industrialized northern hemisphere dictate a profound concern with access to those resources, and with the security of the tanker routes through the Gulf and across the Western Indian Ocean in time of war or political crisis.

Even after the Diego Garcia expansion, our closest comparable capability to that which the Soviets are building at Berbera will be at Subic Bay.
Senator Thurmond: From an operational point of view, which facility, Berbera or Diego Garcia, will be better suited for Indian Ocean operations?
General Brown: They are both well suited. The Soviet position at Berbera is obviously closer to the flow of oil from the Persian Gulf than Diego Garcia and it is also in an excellent position to interdict the flow of commerce through the Red Sea and the newly-opened Suez Canal. . . . The base at Berbera . . . will support and sustain naval combat operations, whereas the facilities that we hope to put on Diego Garcia are far removed from that. They are far less extensive. I would describe Berbera as the initial investment for building a base such as we have at Subic Bay in the Philippines.
Senator Goldwater: How accessible is Berbera to the tanker ship lines of communications from the Persian Gulf to the United States?
General Brown: Berbera is just a few hundred miles to the west of the main shipping line from the Persian Gulf around the east coast of Africa.[137]

In another congressional hearing, former Defense Secretary James R. Schlesinger testified that:

Approximately 85% of the Soviet naval activity has taken place in the Gulf of Aden region, from Aden to Berbera to the Island of Socotra. . . . From the Persian Gulf around the Horn of Africa, around the Cape of Good Hope goes all of the oil from the Middle East to Western Europe and a substantial fraction of our own requirements.[138]

However we interpret Soviet strategy, three facts remain: (1) in Somalia, the Soviets are operating out of their largest military base outside the Warsaw Pact countries; (2) Ethiopia, like Somalia, has become a client

---

[137] U.S. Congress, Senate, *Disapprove Construction Projects on the Island of Diego Garcia*, pp. 21, 23, 27, and 41.

[138] U.S. Congress, House, Committee on International Relations, *Hearings on Diego Garcia: President's Justification for Construction of Limited Facilities on Diego Garcia*, 94th Cong., 1st sess., June 5-November 14, 1975 (Washington, D.C.: GPO, 1975), p. 12. See also, M. Abir, *Sharm al Sheikh and Bab al Mandeb: The Strategic Balance and Israel's Southern Approaches* (Jerusalem: Hebrew University, March 1974).

state of the Soviet Union; and (3) the United States has now become so concerned about Soviet control over Ethiopia and the Horn that President Carter is reported to have ordered Secretary of State Cyrus Vance and National Security Adviser Zbigniew Brzezinski to "move in every possible way to get Somalia to be our friend,"[139] including the offer of arms made on July 25, 1977. This change in U.S. policy rests on the belief that the Soviet Union cannot "ride two horses at the same time"; that, given the long-standing hostility between Ethiopia and Somalia, Moscow will eventually have to choose one over the other. The Kremlin appears to believe that it can ride both horses and will use some form of "federation" of Ethiopia, Somalia and the People's Democratic Republic of Yemen to help accomplish this feat. Whether the USSR is successful or not will be determined largely by the policies and actions of the Sudan, other moderate Arab states, and the United States, and by unfolding developments in the Ogaden and Eritrea.

The Ogaden and Eritrea

The ability of the Soviet Union, demonstrated over a period of many months, to prevent its client, Somalia, from attacking in the Ogaden persuaded Ethiopia to place its future security in Soviet hands. However, once Ethiopia had become a client state, it was no longer essential—as events have proved—to prevent the outbreak of fighting in the Ogaden.[140] In fact, it became important at this stage, if Moscow was to keep Somalia in the fold, to allow this client to resume its campaign to occupy the Ogaden. In carrying out this delicate policy, the Soviets can rely on Ethiopia's desperate need for their support against the Sudan and others in the struggle to retain Eritrea. In fact, it was clear as early as February 1977 that the Derg, in accepting the Soviet proposal for a federation between Somalia and Ethiopia, was disposed to sacrifice the Ogaden, if necessary, in order to retain Eritrea, since it and not the Ogaden provides access to the sea. Given the independence of Djibouti and its pro-Somali government, and the probable early seizure by pro-Somali insurgent forces of Dire Dawa, the rail center in the Ogaden for the railway to Djibouti,[141] Ethiopia's survival depends more than ever on retaining Eritrea.

If the Soviets could now withdraw their support of Ethiopia in the Ogaden to concentrate on saving Eritrea for the Derg, they might be able to achieve four objectives simultaneously: (1) retaining Somalia as a client

---

[139] *Washington Post*, April 26, 1977, p. A-8.

[140] For example, for a report on a raid by 1,500 Somali troops, see the *Washington Post*, February 22, 1977, p. A-14; on the infiltration of 2,000 Somali irregulars in June 1976, see *ibid.*, July 1, 1976.

[141] *Ibid.*, August 3, 1977, p. A-16.

state; (2) retaining Ethiopia as a client state by aiding her in her perilous situation; (3) gaining for themselves footholds on the Eritrean coastline and the islands astride the oil shipping lanes through the Red Sea; and (4) thwarting the aims of the anti-Soviet regime of President Nimeiri of the Sudan, the principal proponent of an independent Eritrea to serve as a buffer between the Sudan and a Soviet Ethiopia. Administering a setback to Nimeiri would be a source of satisfaction to the Soviet Union, which had twice (1971 and 1976) unsuccessfully sought to overthrow him.

On the other hand, since Eritrea is already largely under the control of the ELF-EPLF and the ELF-PLF, an effort to prevent its independence could impose heavy, almost unacceptable burdens on the Soviets. A turn-around in the military situation could probably be achieved only by a campaign of terror and violence surpassing that already indulged in by the Derg. It would also involve a confrontation with the Sudan, supported by Egypt and Saudi Arabia, at a time when the Kremlin seeks to play a key role in the settlement of the Israeli-Arab conflict and to maintain a position of influence in the Middle East. Nor is it likely that the Soviets could gain even a corridor to the sea for Ethiopia through the port of Assab. Such a corridor had been proposed frequently at the meetings of the four great powers, at the Paris Peace Conference and at the UN General Assembly—and rejected. The Somalis and the Djibouti government (so long as it remains independent) would oppose such an outlet as threatening the flow of traffic through Djibouti, and an independent Eritrea certainly would be hostile to Ethiopia and to such a corridor. The Arab states would also resist, since a corridor would have to start at Ras Doumeirah at the present frontier with Djibouti. It is this highly strategic section of coast northward from the Strait of Bab el Mandeb that the Arab League seeks to control.

The loss of Eritrea following upon the loss of the Ogaden and the independence of Djibouti (and perhaps its annexation by Somalia) would almost surely result in the fall of the Derg and the end of Soviet domination. Even the presence of sizable numbers of Cuban troops and the outlay of large financial subsidies to support a rump state entirely cut off from the sea would at best assure the Soviets of a shaky grip on the situation. In such circumstances, the Soviets might opt to withdraw from Ethiopia where, unlike Somalia, it has not yet constructed missile, air or naval bases. It might rationalize the withdrawal in part by calculating that Nimeiri, who came to power with communist support in 1969,[142] might eventually be brought down as a result of a third and successful coup.

---

[142] In August 1969, Nimeiri announced: "We wish to make the new democratic Republic of the Sudan a beacon of Socialism on our continent like the country of Fidel Castro in Latin America." See *Le Monde*, May 17, 1977.

After all, he is opposed today not only by the communists in the Sudan, but also by an impressive following of the arch conservative Mahdi, allied with President Khaddafi of Libya. In that eventuality, an independent Eritrea, largely the creation of Nimeiri, might be swept into the Soviet orbit along with the Sudan. In any event, departure of the Soviets from Ethiopia would free the Sudan, Djibouti and Somalia to seize additional portions of Ethiopia, leaving a truncated and unviable state.

Thus, while the Soviet Union may be capable in the short run of riding two horses at the same time, opportunities do exist to force the Kremlin to withdraw from Ethiopia to its bases and facilities in Somalia.

9.
U.S. Options in the Horn and the Red Sea

T HE DIRECTIVE of President Carter to "move in every possible way to get Somalia to be our friend" and the offer of arms assistance[143] are founded on the optimistic premise that the Soviet Union will be unable to ride both the Somalian and Ethiopian horses and that in the end it will opt in favor of Ethiopia. However, it is difficult to believe that this proposed exchange of Somalia for Ethiopia—if it could be accomplished—would prove beneficial to U.S. interests. Among other things, it would not be particularly advantageous to have the Soviets in control of the western shores of the Red Sea, given the U.S. commitment to guarantee that Israel will receive its normal supplies of oil, pursuant to the Memorandum attached to the 1975 Interim Agreement concerning the Sinai and the Suez Canal.[144]

Regardless of the forms which assistance to Somalia might take,[145] the United States cannot realistically expect to make any headway in expelling the Soviets unless it is prepared to support Somalia on the most fundamental of its objectives—annexation of the Ogaden. It is true that the United States has declared itself in favor of the territorial integrity of Ethiopia, but in fact it has not shown any commitment to this principle in Africa, as its recent position on former Spanish Sahara demonstrates. On the other hand, with respect to the Ogaden, the United States now finds itself in a "no-win" situation: If, as appears more than probable, the Ogaden is seized by Somalia, it is the USSR, not the United States, that would get the credit in Somalia. Moreover, by proposing arms assistance to Somalia at the moment when the Ogaden is all but lost to Ethiopia, the United States obligingly enters as the stalking horse to divert from the Soviets the blame which their client, Ethiopia, would have leveled at them for that loss. Without any tangible benefit to its credit and to the dismay of Israel and Kenya, the United States would have forfeited its options in

---

[143] *Ibid.*, February 28, p. A-20; March 24, p. A-21; April 26, p. A-8; May 17, p. A-13, July 26, p. A-14, 1977.

[144] Paragraphs 3a and 3b of the Israeli-United States Memorandum of Agreement Between the Governments of Israel and the United States: see U.S. Congress, *Congressional Record*, Vol. 121, No. 152, 94th Cong., 1st sess., October 9, 1975, p. S-17969.

[145] The U.S. offer of arms presumes that the Soviets, who control the ports and airports of Kisimayu, Mogadiscio and Berbera, would be so obliging as to permit entry of American munitions, equipment, and perhaps personnel.

Ethiopia and helped to improve the position of the Soviet Union, just at the stage when the latter is being discredited there for the rapid disintegration taking place in the Ogaden, Eritrea and in other provinces of Ethiopia.

Assuming that a Soviet withdrawal from Somalia is less likely than a retreat from the Ethiopian quagmire, the United States might more properly concentrate on an approach to the problem through Eritrea. Both the United States and Israel have an interest in excluding Soviet bases and installations from the Eritrean coast and islands dominating the Red Sea just north of Bab el Mandeb. But Israel, in addition, is opposed to the secession of Eritrea, since its independence would mean that Eritrea, like Djibouti, would become a member of the Arab League and would be dependent upon Arab largesse.

It is here that a dilemma arises for Israel and the United States, for Israel's objectives appear to be mutually exclusive. Israel does not want an Eritrea dominated by the other members of the Arab League. It has dramatically demonstrated the measure of that concern by seeking to help Ethiopia put down the Eritrean revolt—which ironically puts the Israelis in the same boat as the Soviets. Israeli support has taken the form not only of personnel but, much more significantly, of patrol craft operating along the coasts and islands of Eritrea.[146] This Israeli action could lead to two serious consequences that would be detrimental to U.S. and Israeli interests. It could help the Soviets to obtain footholds on the Eritrean coast and islands, and it could undermine the surest route for bringing about the downfall of the Derg and the withdrawal of the Soviet Union, namely, the success of the independence movement in Eritrea.

There is a way out of this dilemma. The movement for Eritrean independence can proceed to the point of causing the Derg's downfall and possibly the withdrawal of the Soviet Union, without irretrievably compromising U.S. and Israeli strategic interests in the Red Sea. The following factors point to a plausible and advantageous solution.

First, except for the three key cities of Asmara, Massawa and Assab, the ELF-EPLF and the ELF-PLF secessionist forces hold all of Eritrea, thanks to the support of the Sudan. It is these forces that constitute the most effective means for bringing down the Derg and convincing the Soviets to withdraw. The largest area of Eritrea—the Western Province, overwhelmingly Muslim and running north of Massawa along the coast to the boundary with the Sudan—is now under the effective control of the ELF-EPLF. The smaller plateau region to the east and the coast from Massawa southward—largely Christian except for the thinly-inhabited Danakil

---

[146] *Wall Street Journal*, July 27, 1977, p. 1.

coast—is largely under the control of the ELF-PLF, although the EPLF forces are strong here, also. All three groups, while Marxist, are anti-Soviet. Because of its identification with the ports and coastal area, the ELF-PLF has expressed hope for U.S. assistance in preventing the Soviets from gaining a foothold in that region and in ensuring freedom of traffic through the Red Sea—a role for the United States that the Israelis could support.

Second, even though Israeli patrols are operating along the Eritrean coast with the approval of the Derg and the Soviet Union, it is reasonable to suppose that the ELF-PLF would prefer the Israeli presence there to that of the Soviets. Pending a final solution to the Eritrean problem, Israel might take advantage of this conjuncture to take over the defense of the Eritrean ports of Assab and Massawa, the offshore archipelago of Dahlac, the uninhabited Hanish-Zuqar group in mid-sea, and the lighthouse islands of Abu Ail and Jebel Tair administered from Massawa.

Third, a noncommunist alternative to the Derg—the Ethiopian Democratic Union (EDU)—is available and should be given assistance so that it is ready to assume power when the Derg collapses. So far, the United States has failed in this respect, apparently chiefly out of concern for the safety of the 400 Americans still in Ethiopia. However, after cutting off arms shipments to Ethiopia early in 1977 and offering arms to Ethiopia's enemy, Somalia, this "non-involvement" policy scarcely seems credible. While it is legitimate to question whether the EDU is an ideal alternative, it is at least the best one in existence. The United Kingdom has not hesitated to establish contact with that organization despite the presence of British nationals in Ethiopia. The United States has been so timid that it has even refused asylum, with certain rare exceptions, to Ethiopians seeking to flee from the cruelties of the Derg—yet it had previously cut off arms to Ethiopia for precisely that reason. Were the United States to take as strong a stand on this issue as Britain, Sweden, France, West Germany and Italy have, U.S. opposition to the pro-Soviet Derg would be more convincing.

Fourth, the Sudan is uniquely situated to influence the course of events in Ethiopia and Eritrea. It has traditionally had close and confident relations with Ethiopia, the source of 80 per cent of its water.[147] Until the abortive coup of July 1976 against President Nimeiri, in which the Derg is

---

[147] All Sudanese leaders—Khalil, Al Azhari, Abboud, Magoub, Nimeiri—were on intimate consultative terms with the leaders of pre-Derg Ethiopia. The Sudan is faced with problems in the South similar to those confronting Ethiopia in Eritrea. The Christian South has long sought autonomy from the Muslim North. Ironically, it was the Christian Emperor of Ethiopia that came to the rescue of the Muslim government of the Sudan by ordering an air lift of arms and the transportation of Sudanese troops by Ethiopian Airlines for suppressing a revolt in the South in 1955. Yet, just as ironically, it is the Christian element in southern Sudan that opposes the secessionist movement in Eritrea because it sees there the possibility of another Muslim triumph.

alleged to have conspired with Libya, the Sudan had opposed the secessionist movement in Eritrea, fearing that it might serve as a precedent for its own, largely Christian, southern region—which has long threatened to secede and which opposes independence for Eritrea, fearing Moslem domination of the Christian highlands. Mindful of that danger, the Sudan had carried its opposition to the point that it had cooperated with Ethiopia in suppressing the influx of arms to the insurgents from other Arab states, and had mediated efforts to achieve a solution of the Eritrean question within a framework of local autonomy.

Since the abortive coup of July 1976 and the Sovietization of Ethiopia, however, the Sudan has supported not only the ELF and the EPLF in Eritrea, but also the Ethiopian EDU, by arms, radio propaganda and funds, and by providing asylum for some 200,000 troops and refugees from Ethiopia, including many Eritreans.

The Sudan, along with Egypt and Saudi Arabia, views with deep concern the existence of a pro-Soviet regime in Ethiopia, dependent for its survival on Soviet power.[148] Its present support of the independence movement is, therefore, motivated by the felt need to create a buffer state between itself and a Soviet Ethiopia. With the removal of that regime, the Sudan might well revert to its traditional concern to prevent secessionist movements in its neighborhood along with its mediation efforts toward gaining autonomy for Eritrea within Ethiopia. Continued Sudanese support of the EDU is evidence of the survival of that traditional policy. Yet it would be unrealistic to suppose that autonomy for Eritrea along the lines proposed earlier by the Sudan could apply today after so much blood has been spilled in Eritrea's secessionist struggle. Any formula for autonomy would have to require the withdrawal of all Ethiopian troops, except for a token presence.

As past debates at the UN General Assembly over the future of Eritrea have made clear, that area is not economically viable, and its fierce resistance against Addis Ababa in 1976 and 1977 has been dependent upon Arab assistance, especially from the Sudan. Under the circumstances, independence for Eritrea might be a fleeting experience; hence, a formula for partitioning and autonomy might provide the best solution to the Eritrean question.

The formula of autonomy within Ethiopia might be applied to the area of the plateau which is largely Christian and to the adjoining Danakil coast running from Massawa to the Strait of Bab el Mandeb. It is in this area where the ELF-PLF seeks U.S. support against Soviet encroachment, and where, under the suggestion made above, Israel would have been invited

---

[148] In May 1977, the Sudan expelled 90 Soviet military advisers and ordered the closing of the military section of the Soviet Embassy. *New York Times*, May 19, 1977, p. A-7.

to establish its presence in the ports and on the coastal and mid-sea islands. A solution along the lines of autonomy for this area would also satisfy the Sudan, because of the precedent it would set for its own Christian south. This region is also heavily dependent on the adjoining and more fertile Ethiopian province of Tigre and intimately identified with it culturally and linguistically.

The much larger area of the Western Province is overwhelmingly Moslem and presents a much different problem. While independence could prove to be an attractive symbol and objective for the ELF-EPLF, it would be totally unrealistic for an area characterized largely by grazing and sparse agriculture. Attachment of this area to the Sudan would make a great deal of sense. It is of interest to note that, in the discussion of the Eritrean question at the General Assembly in 1949, Egypt proposed that this area be annexed by the Sudan. That proposal was defeated by the votes of the Soviet and Latin American blocs and opposed by the dominant ethnic group in the region, which did not view with favor the possibility of domination by the neighboring Hadendowa of the Sudan.´

Today, however, the violence and the atrocities which the Derg has inflicted on the inhabitants of the Western Province have undoubtedly altered the attitudes of a quarter of a century ago. In fact, a substantial part of that population has already taken refuge in the Sudan. Certainly the Sudan has not forgotten the claim made on its behalf at the General Assembly. The transfer of the Western Province to the Sudan would make it easier for Khartoum to accept a formula of autonomy for the rest of Eritrea within Ethiopia. The Sudan would gain an important stretch of coastline on the Red Sea without depriving Ethiopia of the essential ports of Massawa and Assab. Moreover, it is precisely that northern stretch of the Eritrean coast that lies opposite the shores of Saudi Arabia. With its acquisition by an Arab Muslim state, Saudi Arabia would have less cause to oppose the two-part solution of partition and autonomy.

If the EDU accepts such a solution, announces the return of the ports of Massawa and Assab, and pledges to work with the Sudan in implementing the plan as soon as the Derg can be overthrown, the peoples of Ethiopia might well rally to the EDU in support of such a solution, preferring it to the loss of all of Eritrea following the annexation of both the Ogaden and Djibouti by Somalia. An intensification of the struggle by the Ethiopian and Eritrean insurgents against the Derg and its Soviet backers could lead to the intervention of Cuban mercenaries, but the latter would soon discover that they were in a struggle against all but one (the People's Democratic Republic of Yemen) of the Arab states bordering on the Red Sea.

A formula for retaining a portion of Eritrea within Ethiopia is not sufficient by itself, however, to uproot the present pro-Soviet regime. The

Sudan must play its key role, and so must the EDU or some more viable grouping which would replace it; and both will need political support from the United States, which has been lacking to date. This requires a change in the traditional American policy of non-involvement. Troop commitments, as in the case of Korea, are out of the question and probably would be counterproductive. But some limited measures should be taken to break with the traditional hands-off policy which the United States has applied to Africa. The Sudan should, at the minimum, have the benefit of a Liberian-type agreement by which the United States would put others on notice that (in the words of the U.S.-Liberian agreement), "In the event of aggression or threat of aggression against the Sudan, the Government of the United States of America and the Government of the Sudan will immediately determine what action may be appropriate for the defense of the Sudan." Such assurance, which the United States never gave Ethiopia, should also be made available to any pro-Western regime that comes to power in Ethiopia, and it might be offered to Kenya as well.

10.
Summary and Conclusions

THE WEAKNESS in the U.S. position comes from blindly pursuing two traditional policies. The first has been to assume that the long-standing policy of avoiding strategic commitments in Africa requires Washington also to forswear political influence there. The second has been to treat Ethiopian problems as essentially African rather than Middle Eastern. Both policies are in fundamental error.

The United States has been in position for more than 40 years to exert political influence in the Horn but has failed from the start to act in conformance with its own interests and assessments. In 1936 it accepted the League of Nations decision that the Ogaden was part of Ethiopia. In 1944 and again in 1946 it took the view that Britain should not seek to annex the Ogaden for the purpose of creating a Greater Somaliland—an exogenous movement of British inspiration. Had the United States adhered to its position on the Ogaden and exerted its political influence, the crisis in the Horn could have been avoided in later years. On the contrary, by exacerbating the problem in 1959—when it provided cover to the British in promoting the union of British and Italian Somalilands—the United States laid the basis for the eventual Soviet takeover of the Horn in 1977. Neither the Soviet build-up in Somalia nor Ethiopia's desperate surrender to the Soviet Union would have been possible without the abiding presence of the Ogaden issue.

The United States, which in the 1950s and early 1960s enjoyed a position of unparalleled prestige and influence in Ethiopia and the Horn, now finds itself replaced by the Soviet Union and ill-prepared to cope with the communist threat to take over the entire Horn. If the Soviets secure this vantage point, they would be able to exert new pressures on states to the north in the Nile valley and to the west and south in black Africa; on the states of the Middle East in general, including Israel; on the Indian Ocean and Persian Gulf regions; and ultimately on Western Europe.

The United States failed to develop, with its NATO allies, long-term policies that would provide solutions to the serious economic and political problems of the Horn. Nothing seemed to stir the United States out of its serene postwar contemplation of the region, despite the mounting crises of the Greater Somaliland Movement, the steady growth of Soviet military and political influence in the Horn, the Soviet and radical Arab subversion in Eritrea, and the steady and inexorable decline of the Ethiopian monarchy. During this same period, the United States fought communist forces, proxies and subversion in many areas of the globe—in Greece, Berlin, Korea, Guatemala, Cuba, Vietnam and elsewhere—but never acknowledged that Africa could be a primary target of Soviet global strategy or that the Horn could have substantial strategic interest for the United States.

The Soviet Union, on the other hand, has had the strategic vision to see the significance of the Horn. Somalia now contains the largest Soviet missile base outside Europe and Asia. Not only has the USSR supplanted the United States in Ethiopia, but it has transformed both Ethiopia and Somalia into client states. In 1936, Ethiopia was merged with Eritrea and Somalia into a fascist Horn of Africa. It is a measure of Ethiopia's surrender to the Soviet Union that in 1977 the Derg has publicly embraced Moscow's proposal to revert to the solution of forty years ago—a merger of Ethiopia with Somalia and Eritrea. This time, however, it is not a fascist, but the Soviet Horn of Africa that is being created.

Confronted with the prospect of Soviet denial-control over the northwest quadrant of the Indian Ocean, the Horn and the Red Sea, President Carter has determined that the United States must now "move in every possible way to get Somalia to be our friend." The desperation and futility of the proposal reveal the degree of concern and frustration. While the new Administration cannot be held responsible for decades of Ethiopian misrule and U.S. miscalculation, it is responsible for the future of American policy. There is still time for the United States to assist the noncommunist forces in the area to join together in blocking a total Soviet takeover of the Horn.

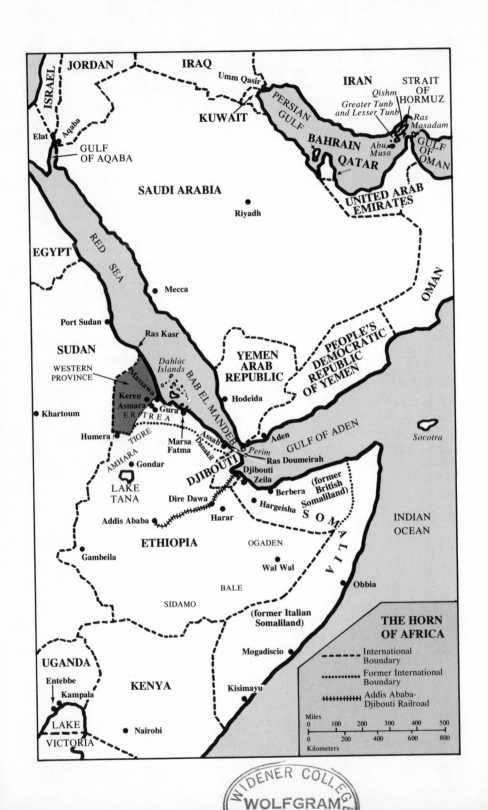

THE HORN
OF AFRICA

- – – International Boundary
- • • • • • Former International Boundary
- +++++ Addis Ababa-Djibouti Railroad

Miles
0   100   200   300   400   500
0   200   400   600   800
Kilometers